DON'T STRANGLE THEM! THEY'RE JUST STUPID. HERE COLOR THIS INSTEAD!

AN ADULT COLORING BOOK TO CALM THE ANGRY STRESS FILLED MIND.

VOLUME 1.
ANIMALS, FLORAL DESIGNS, AND ABSTRACT PATTERNS.

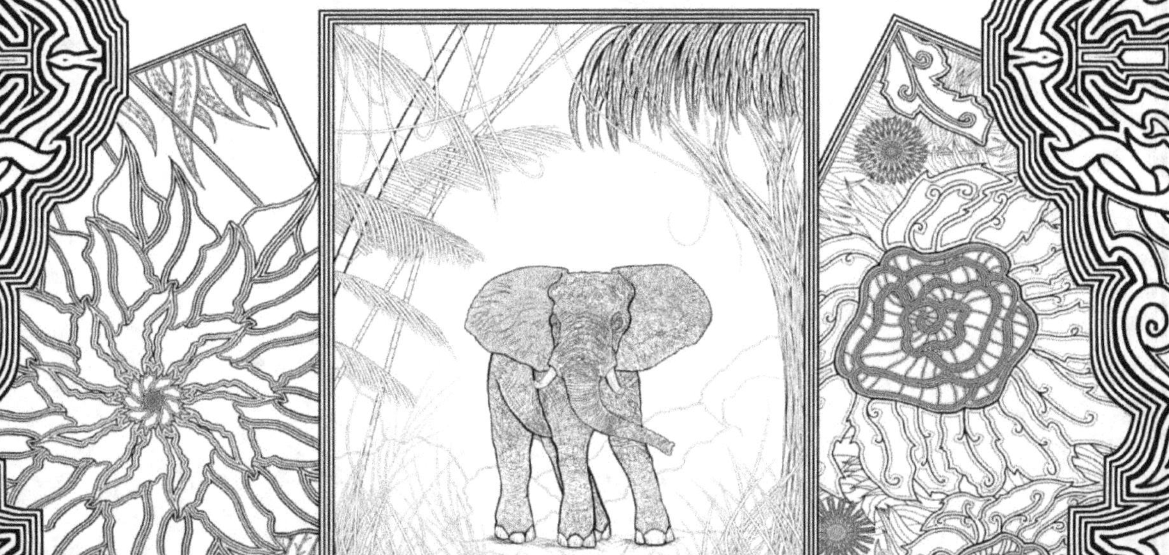

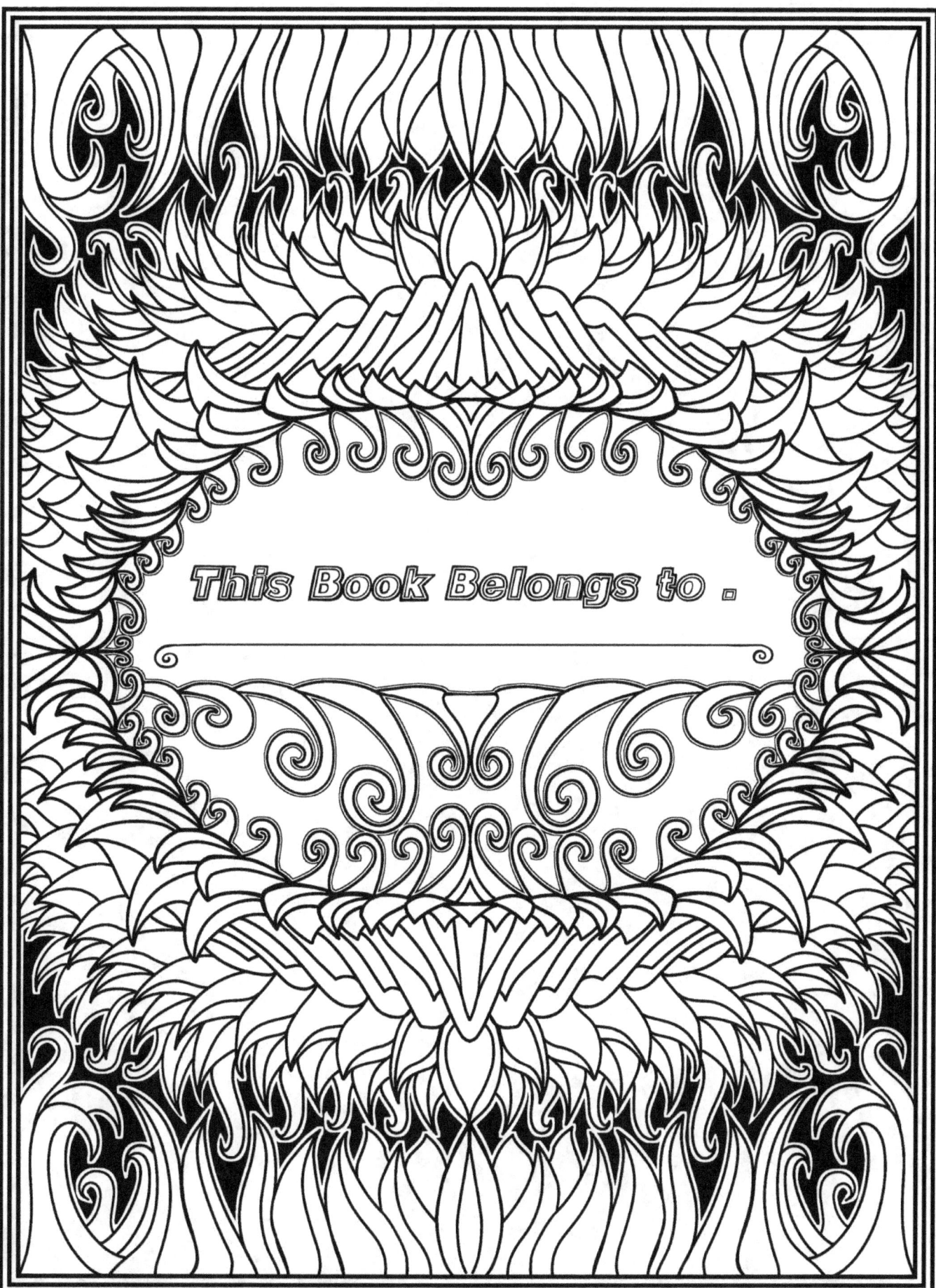

This Book Belongs to .

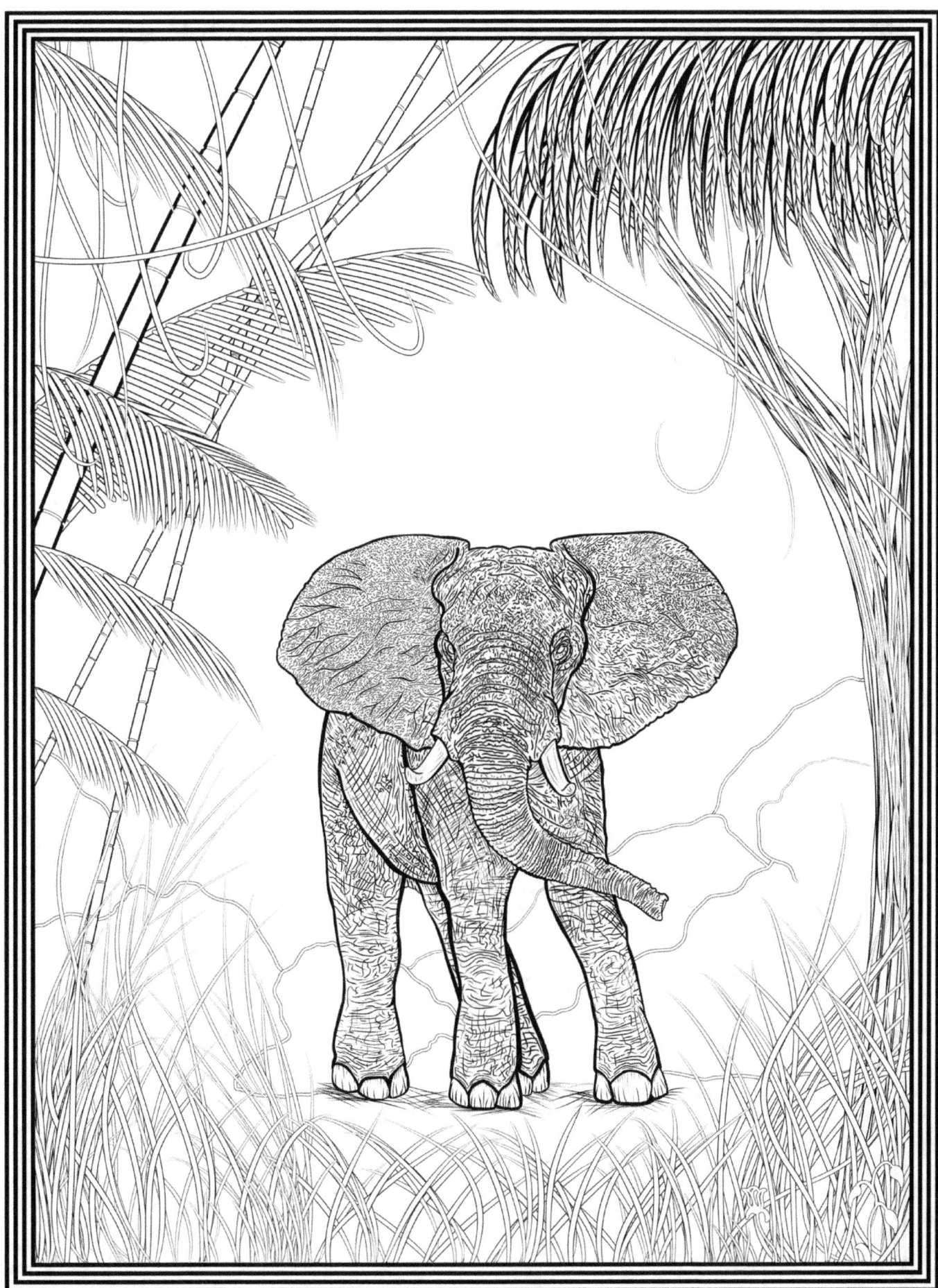

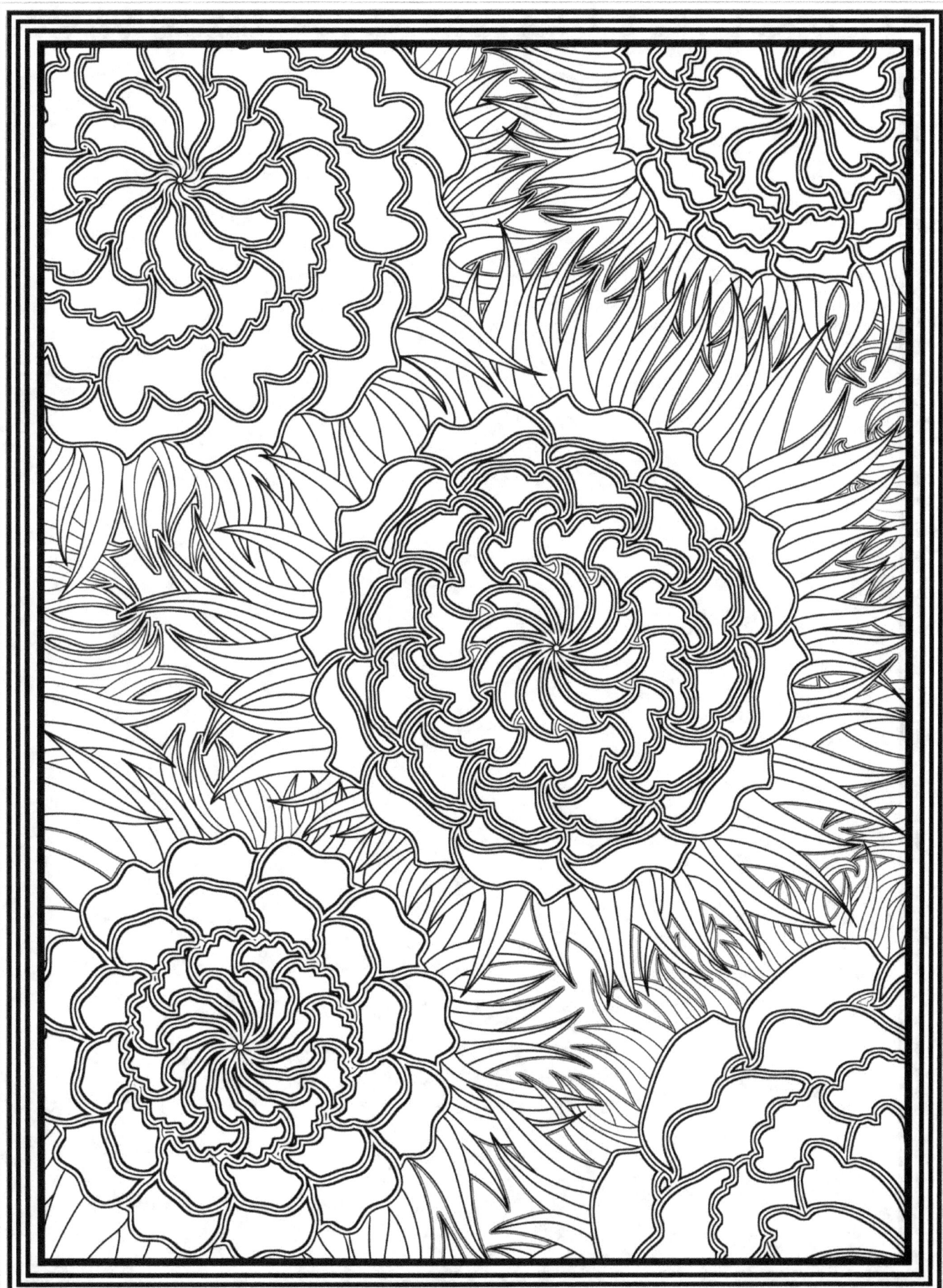

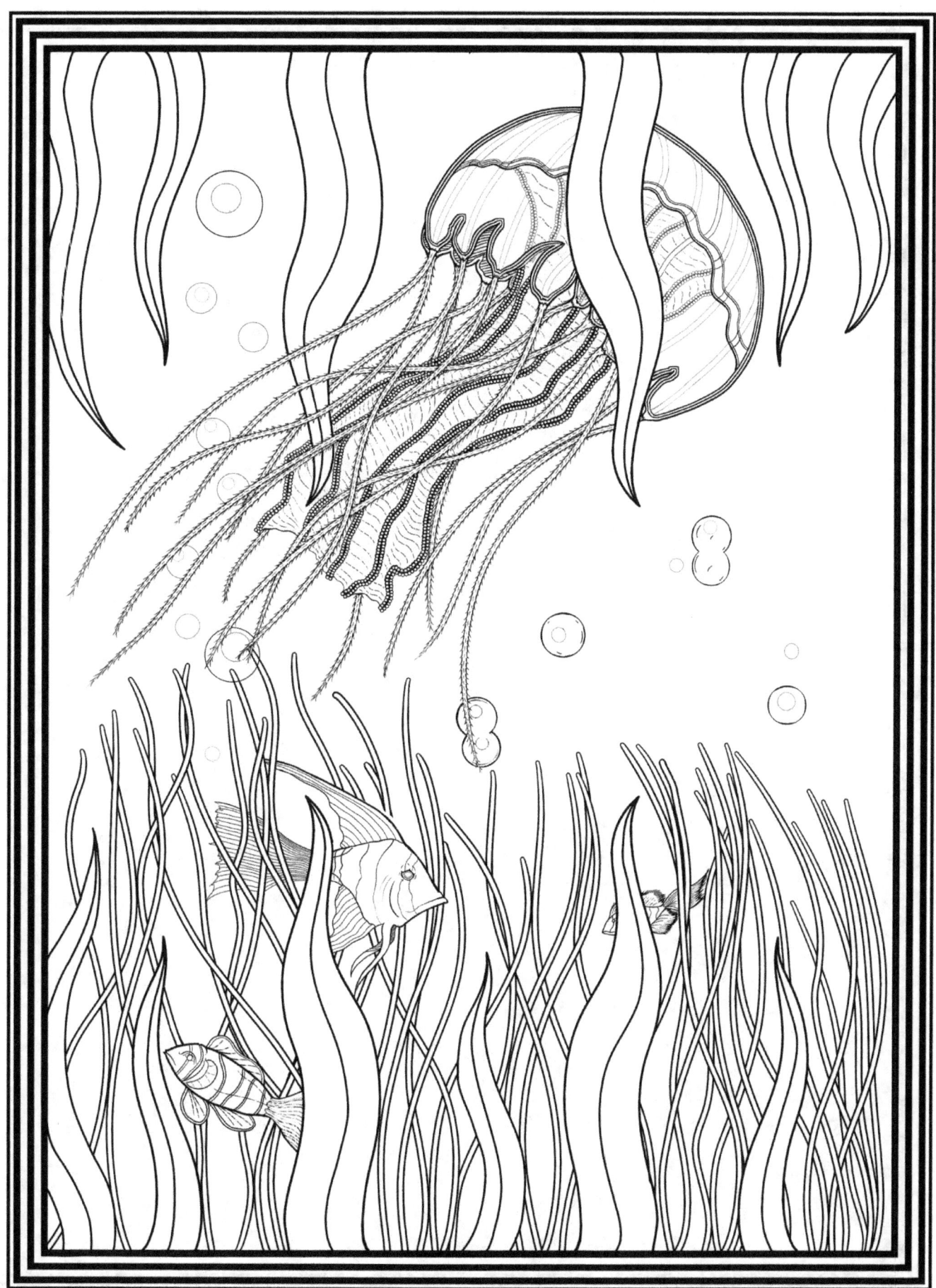

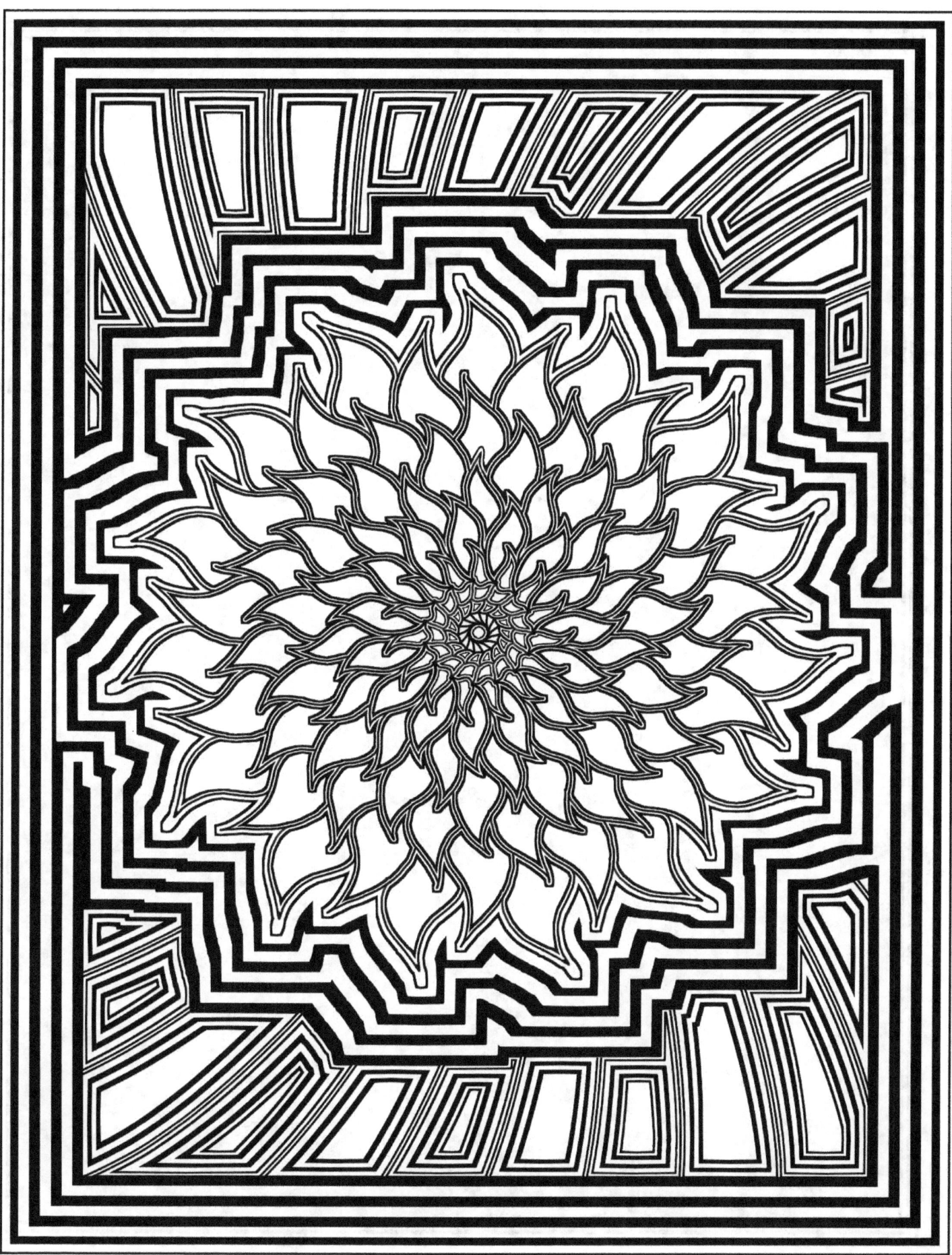

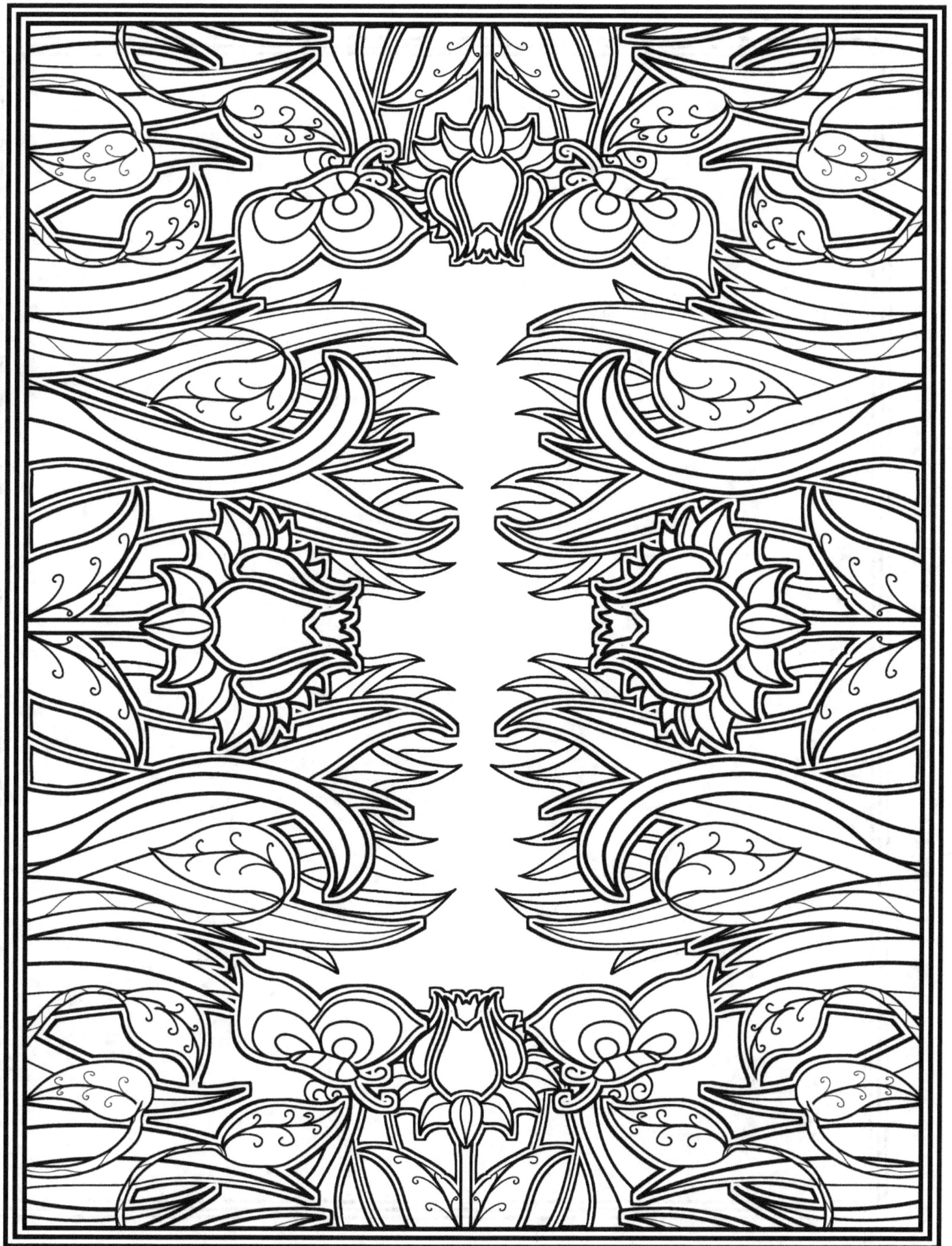

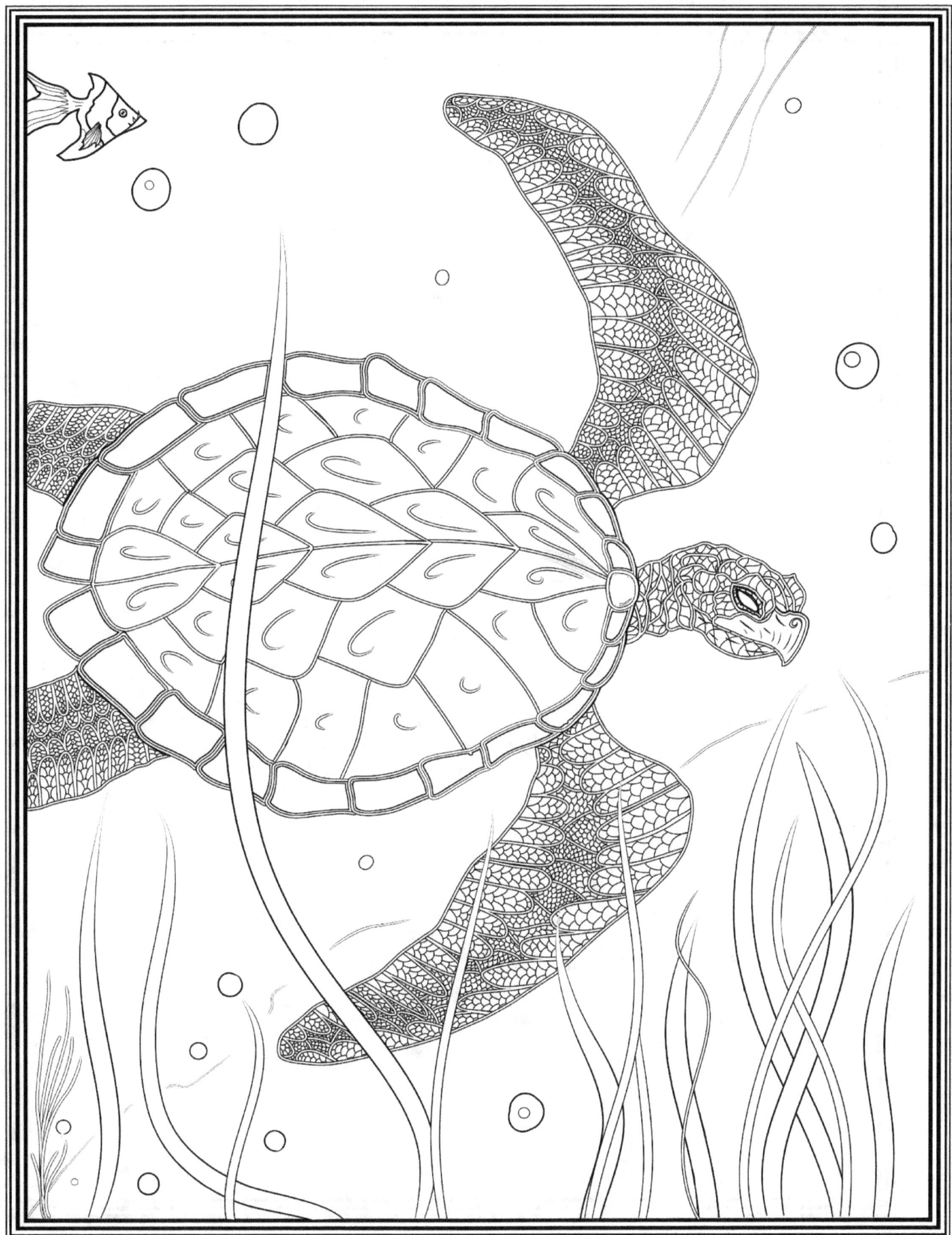

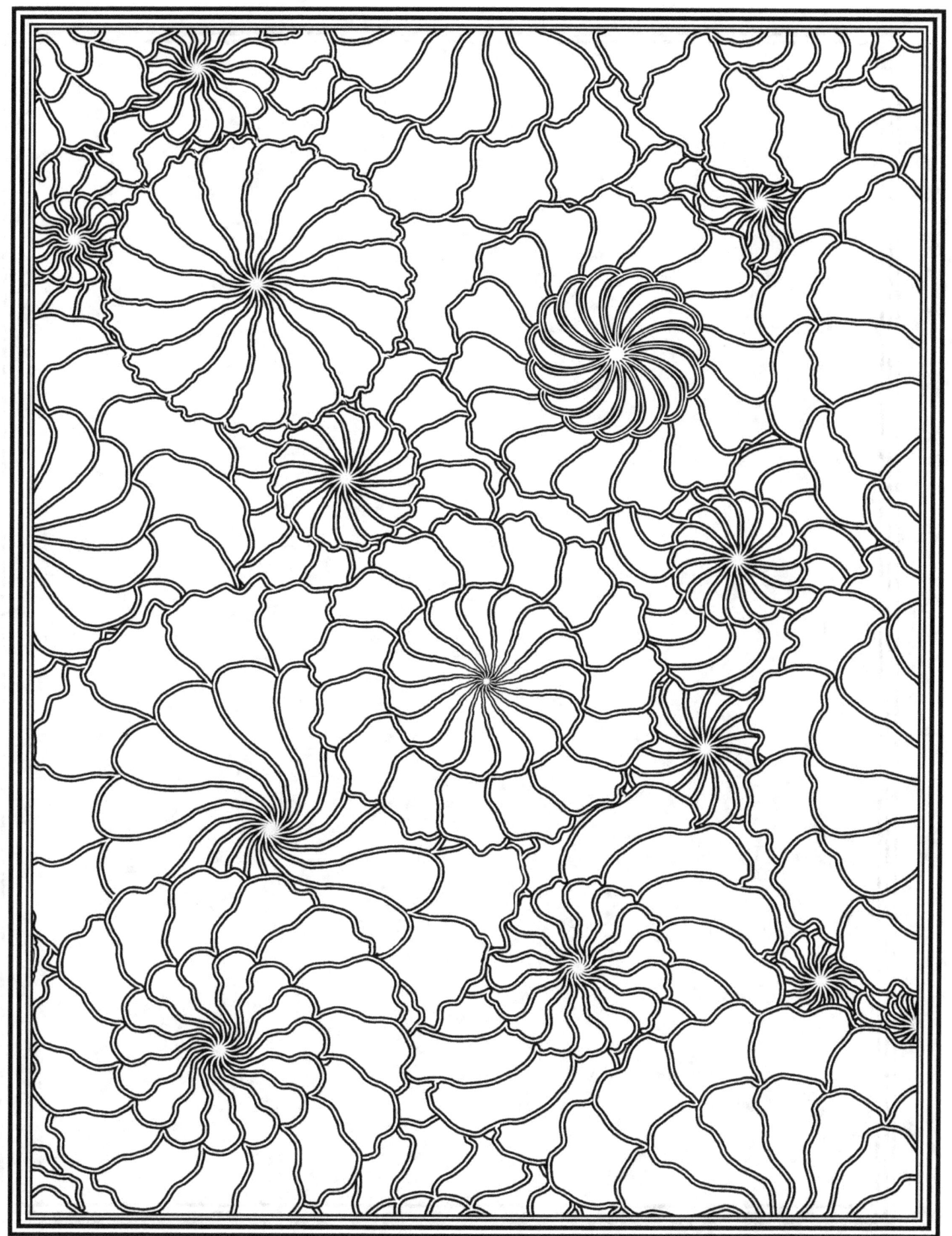

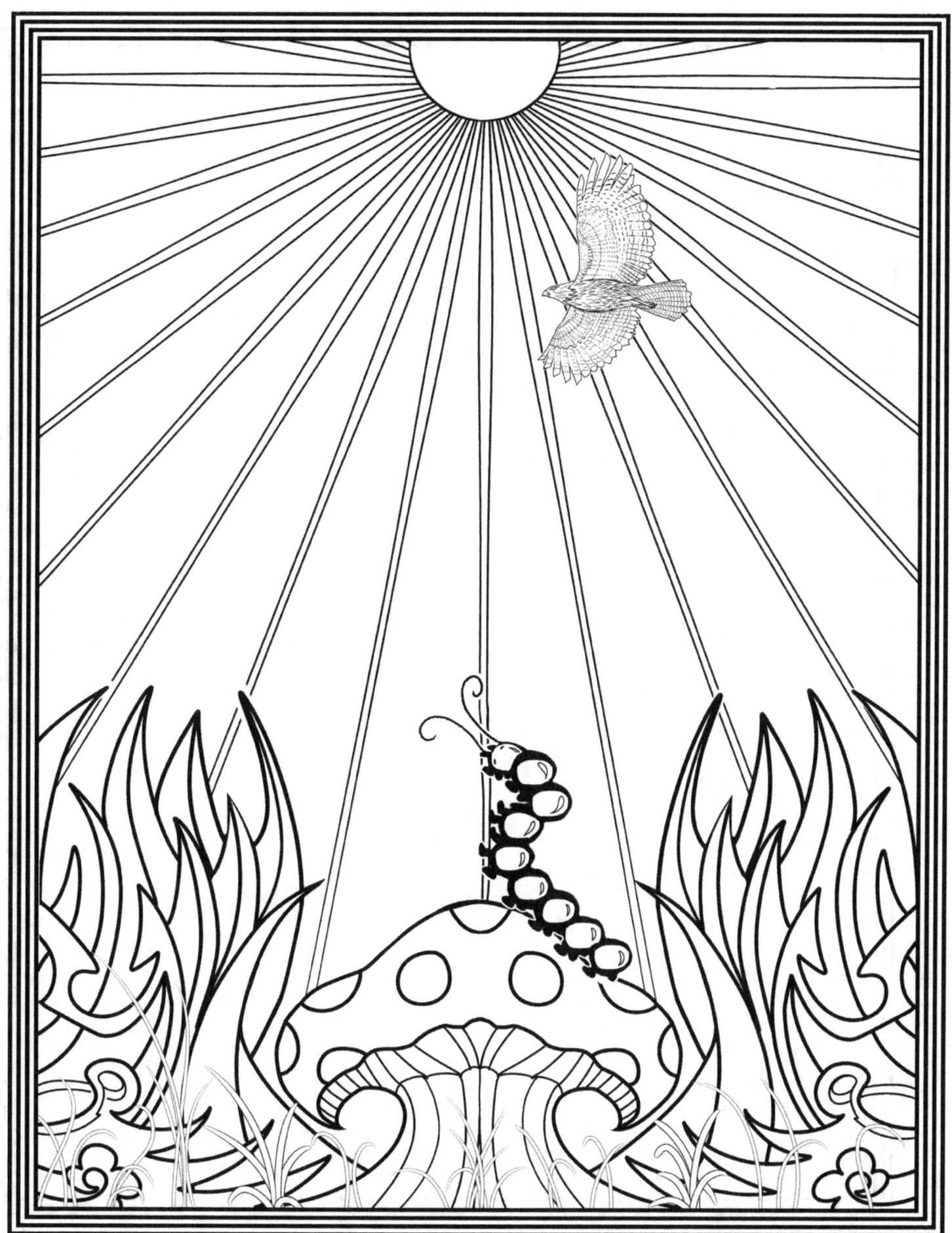

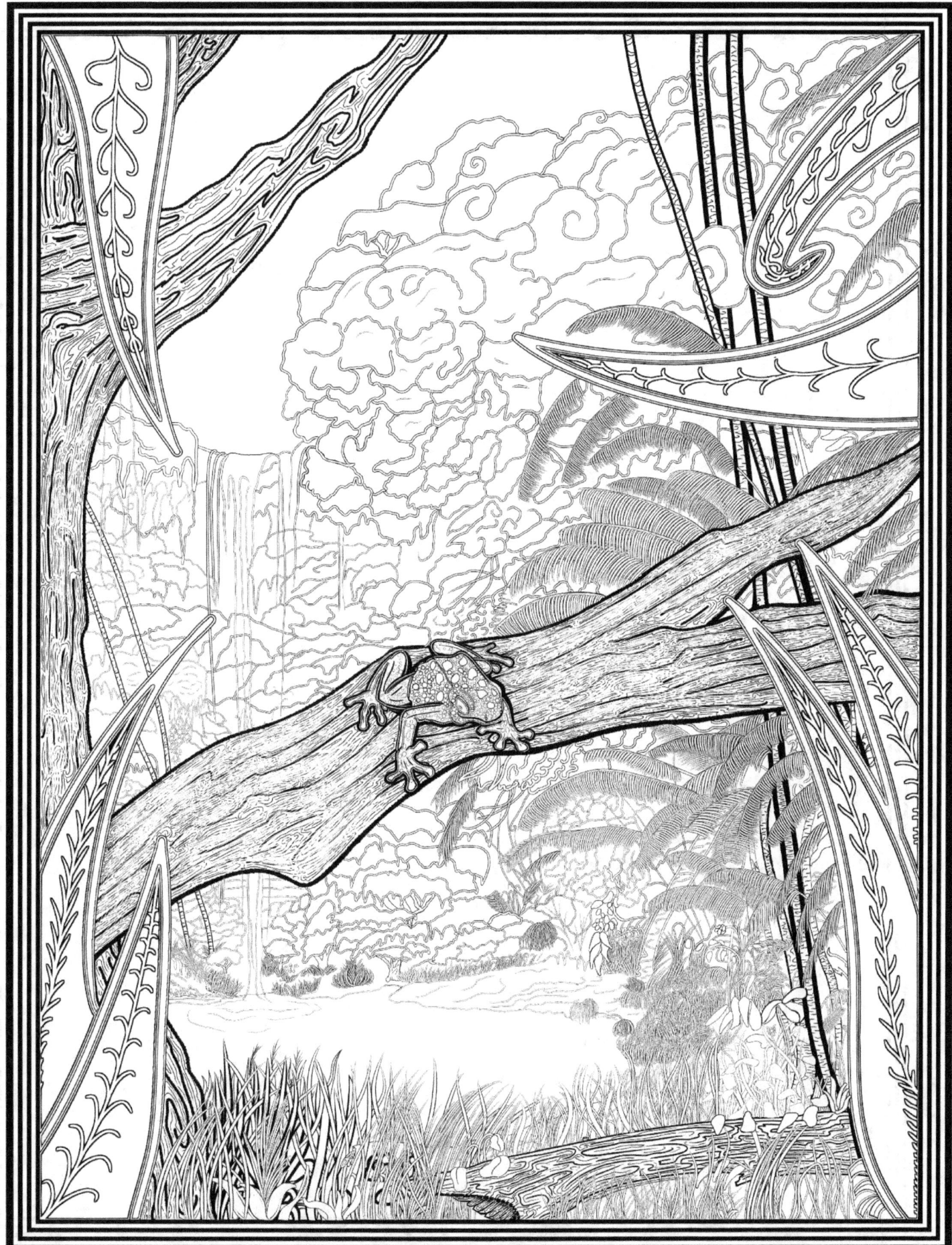

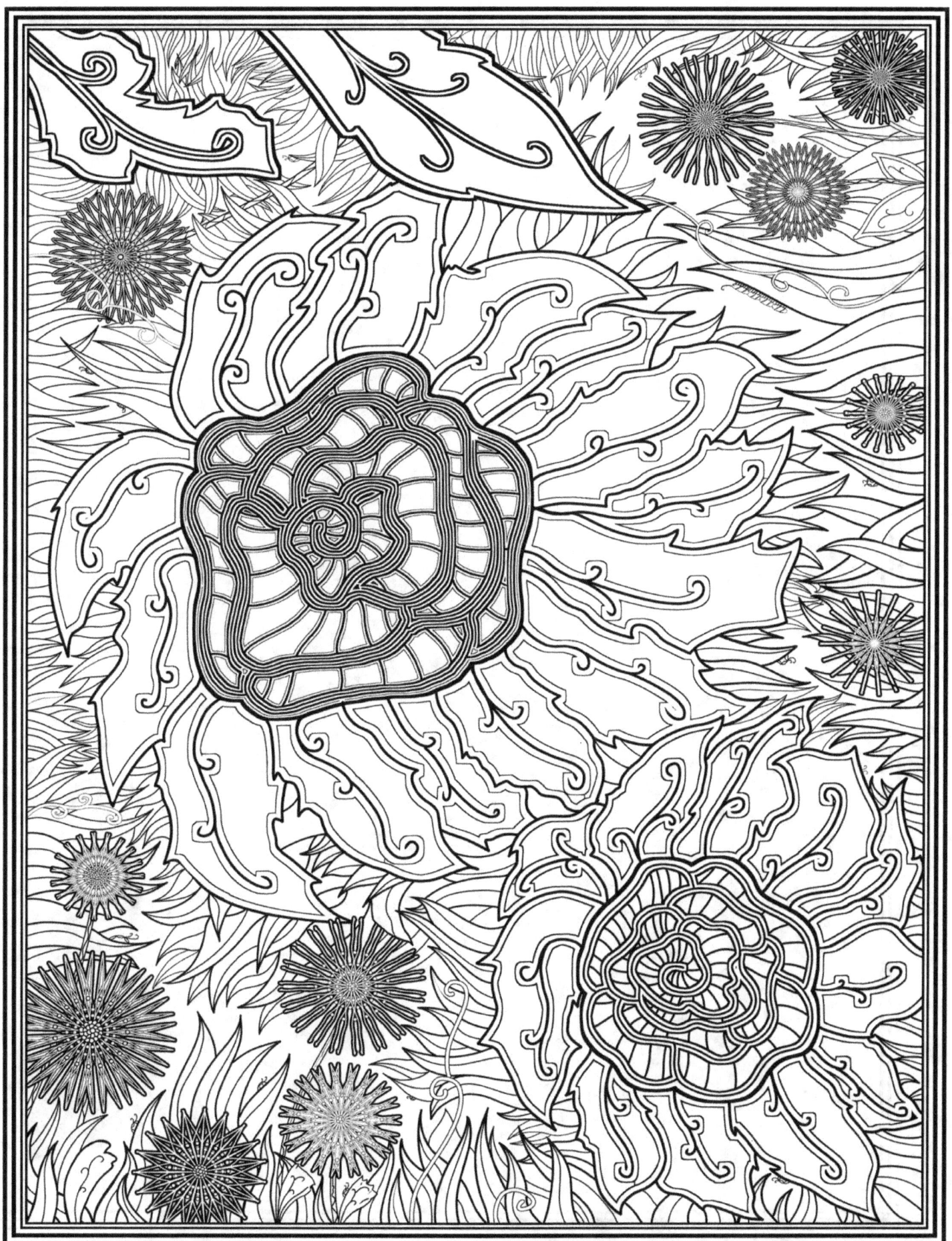

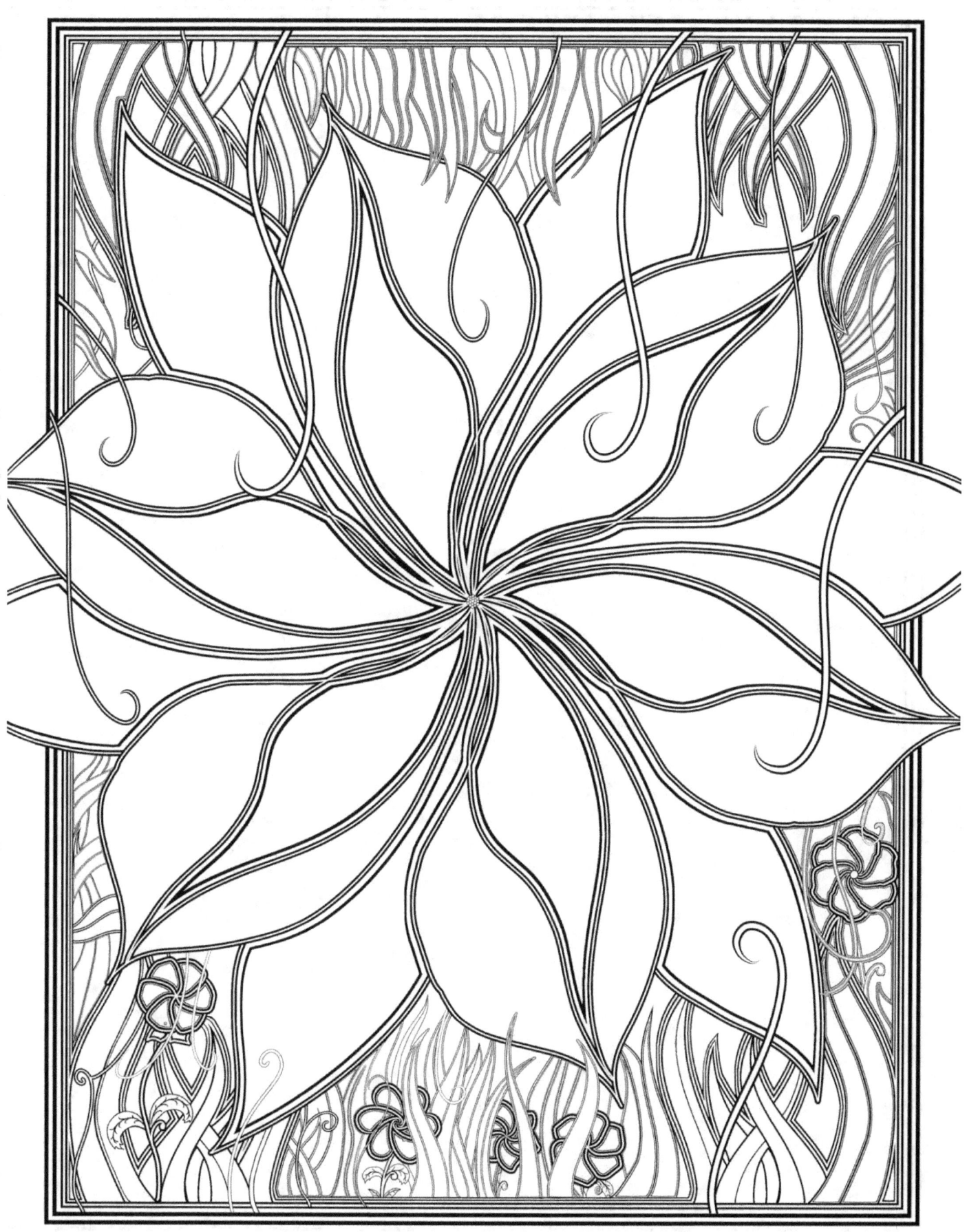

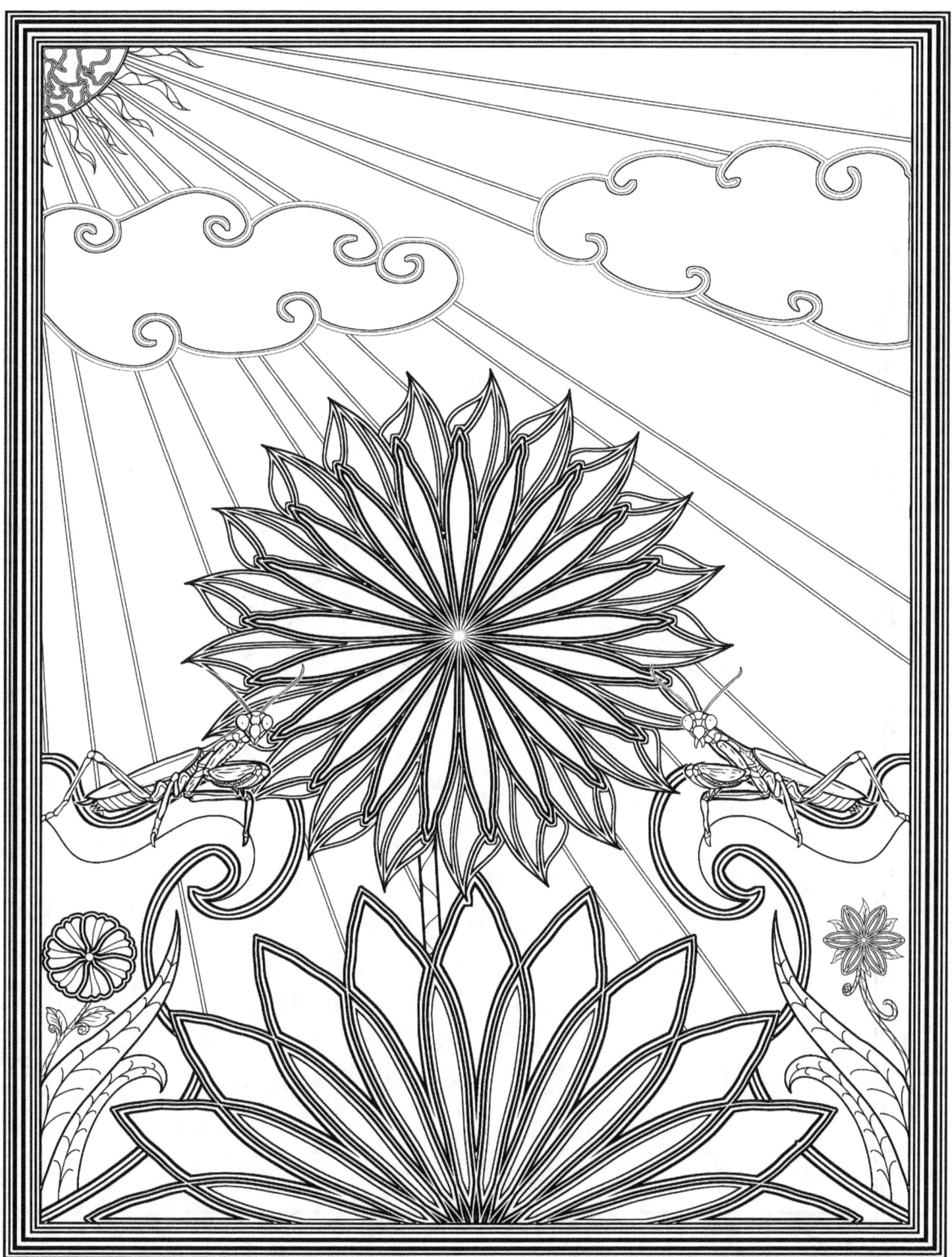

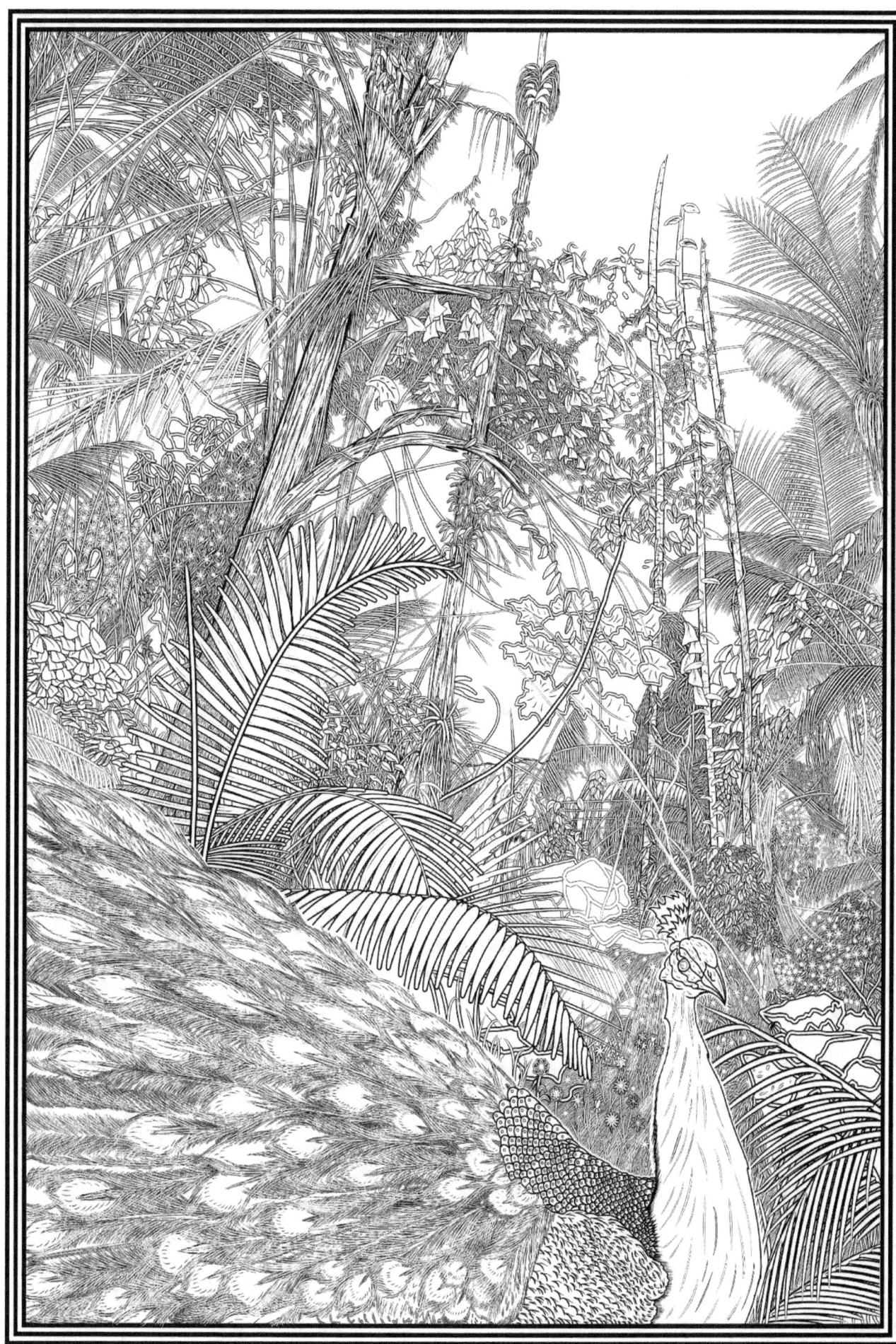

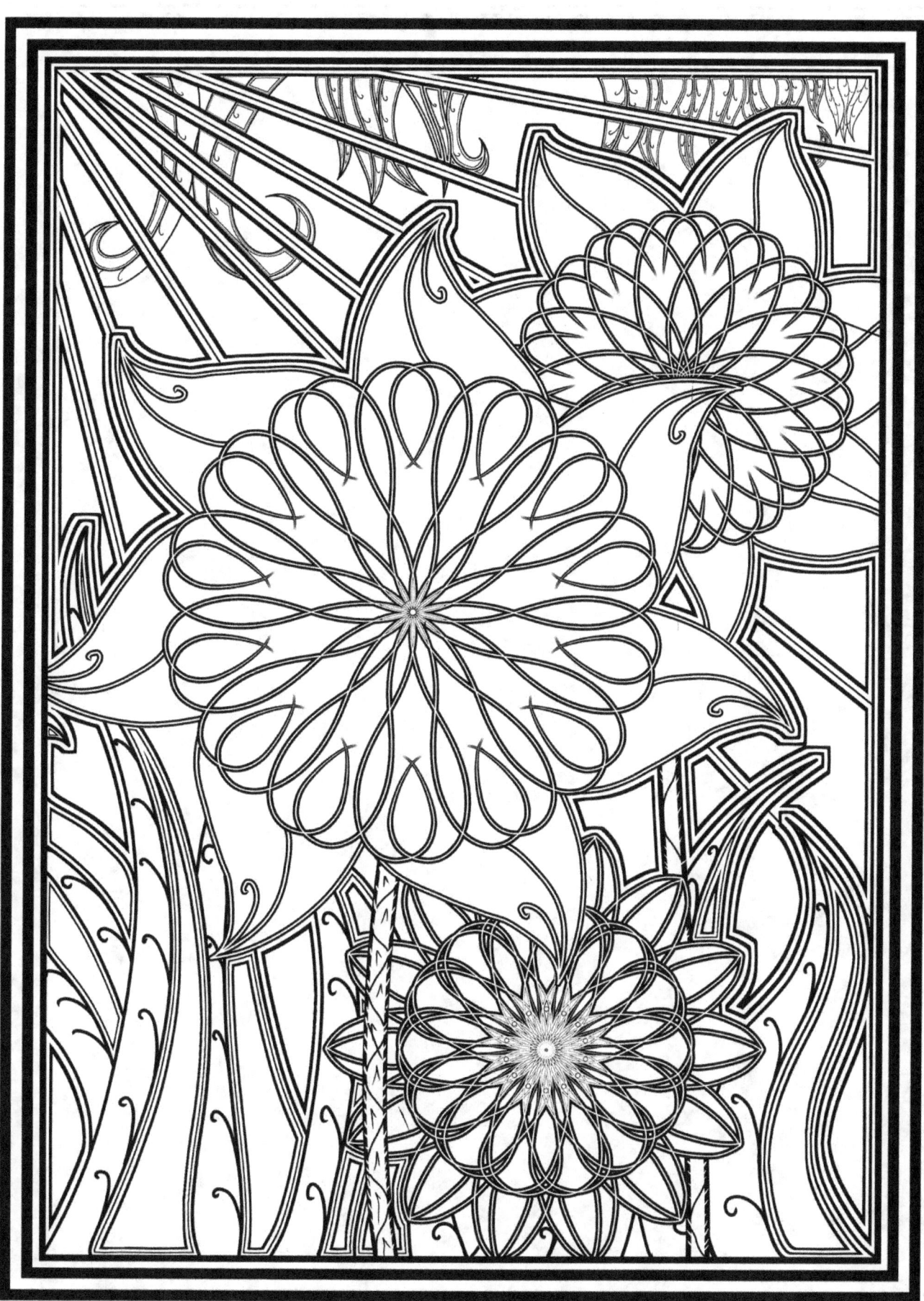

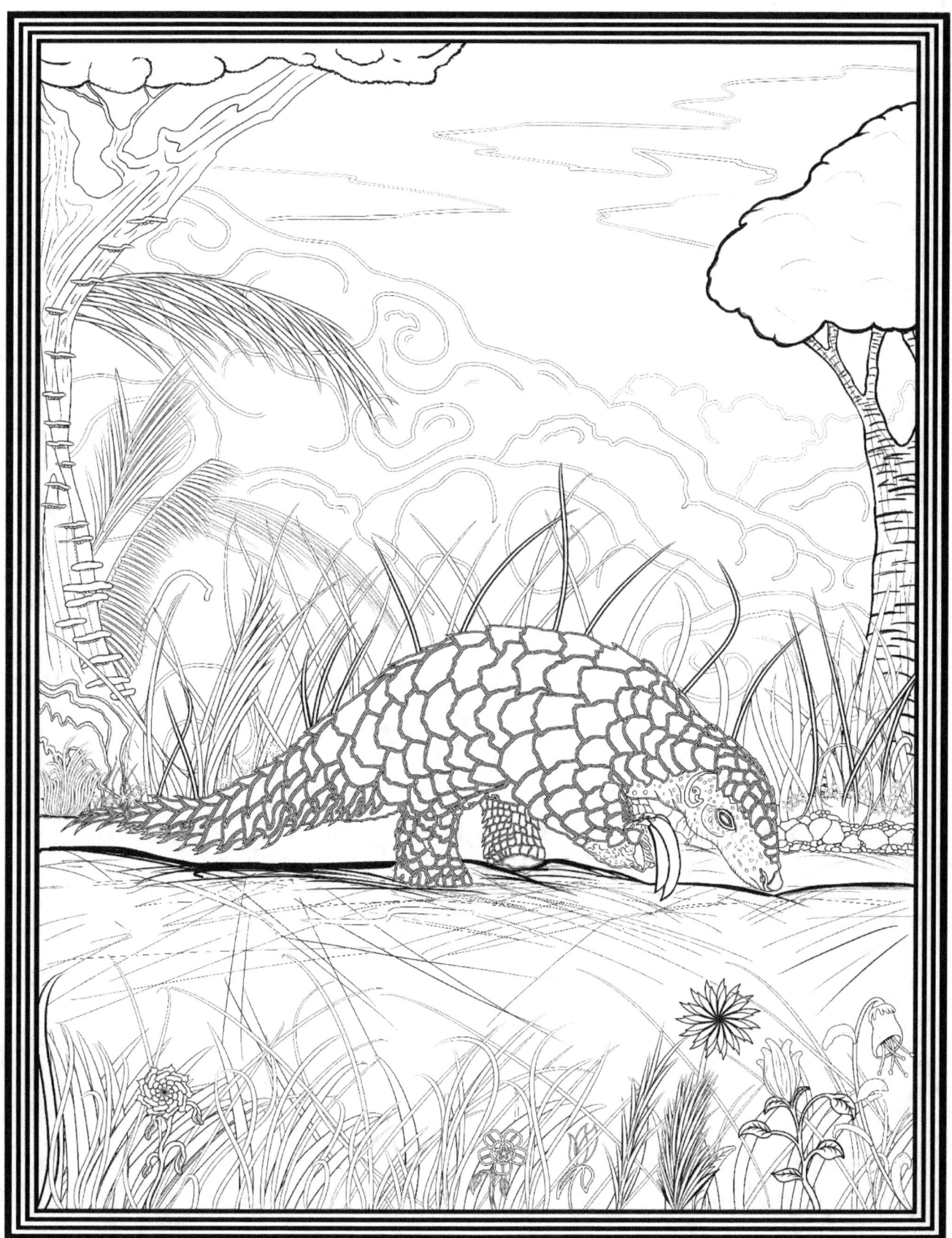

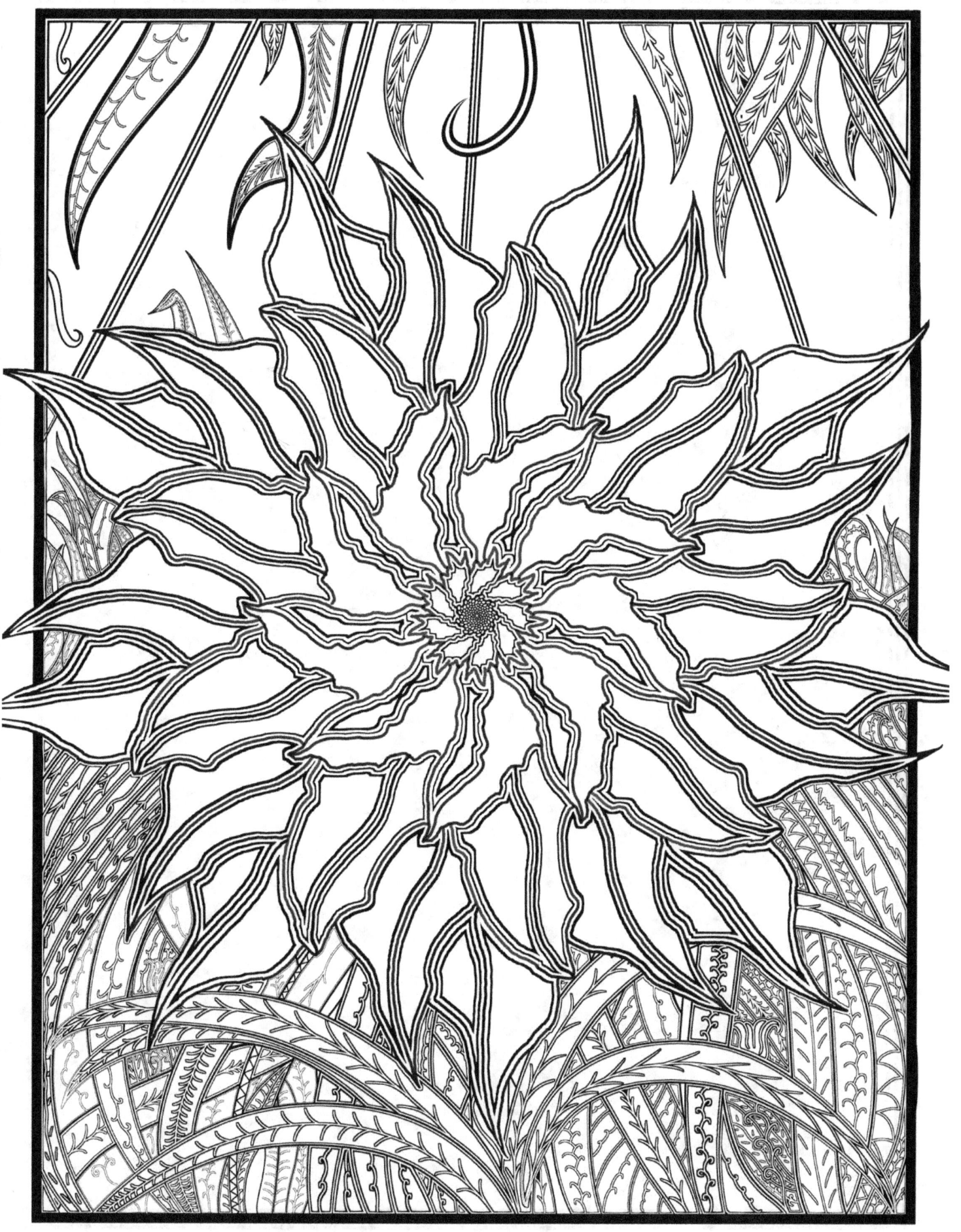

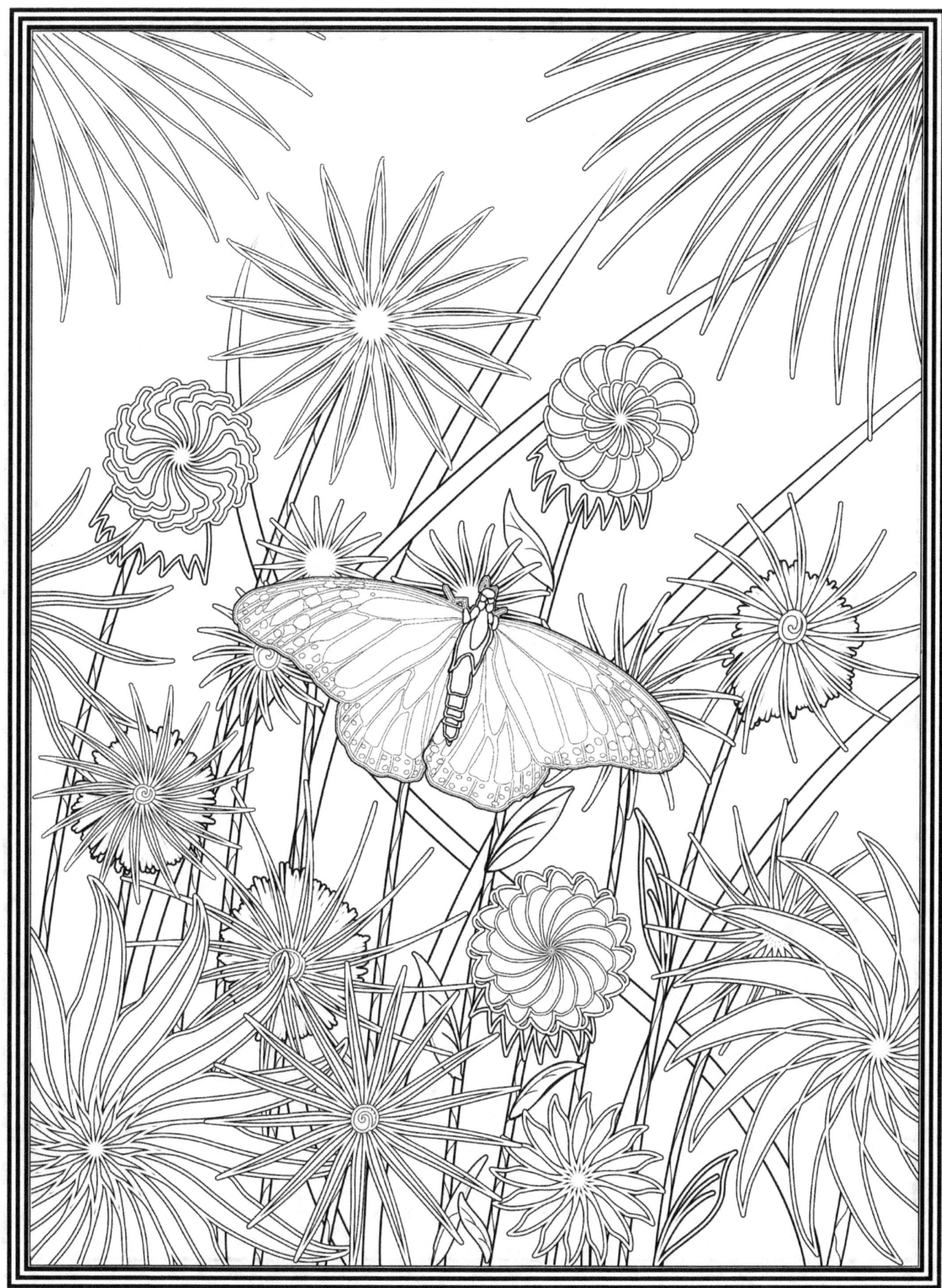

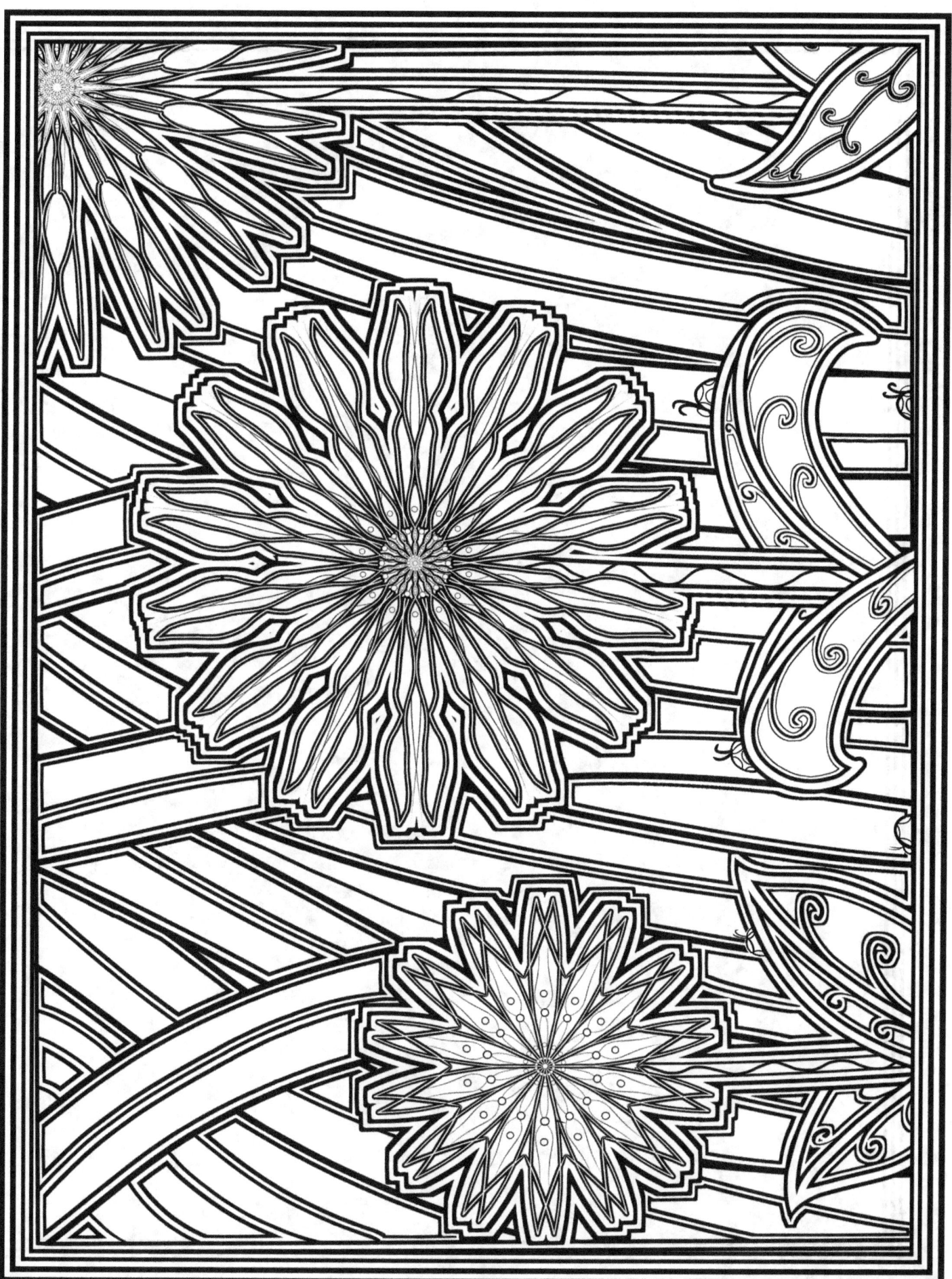

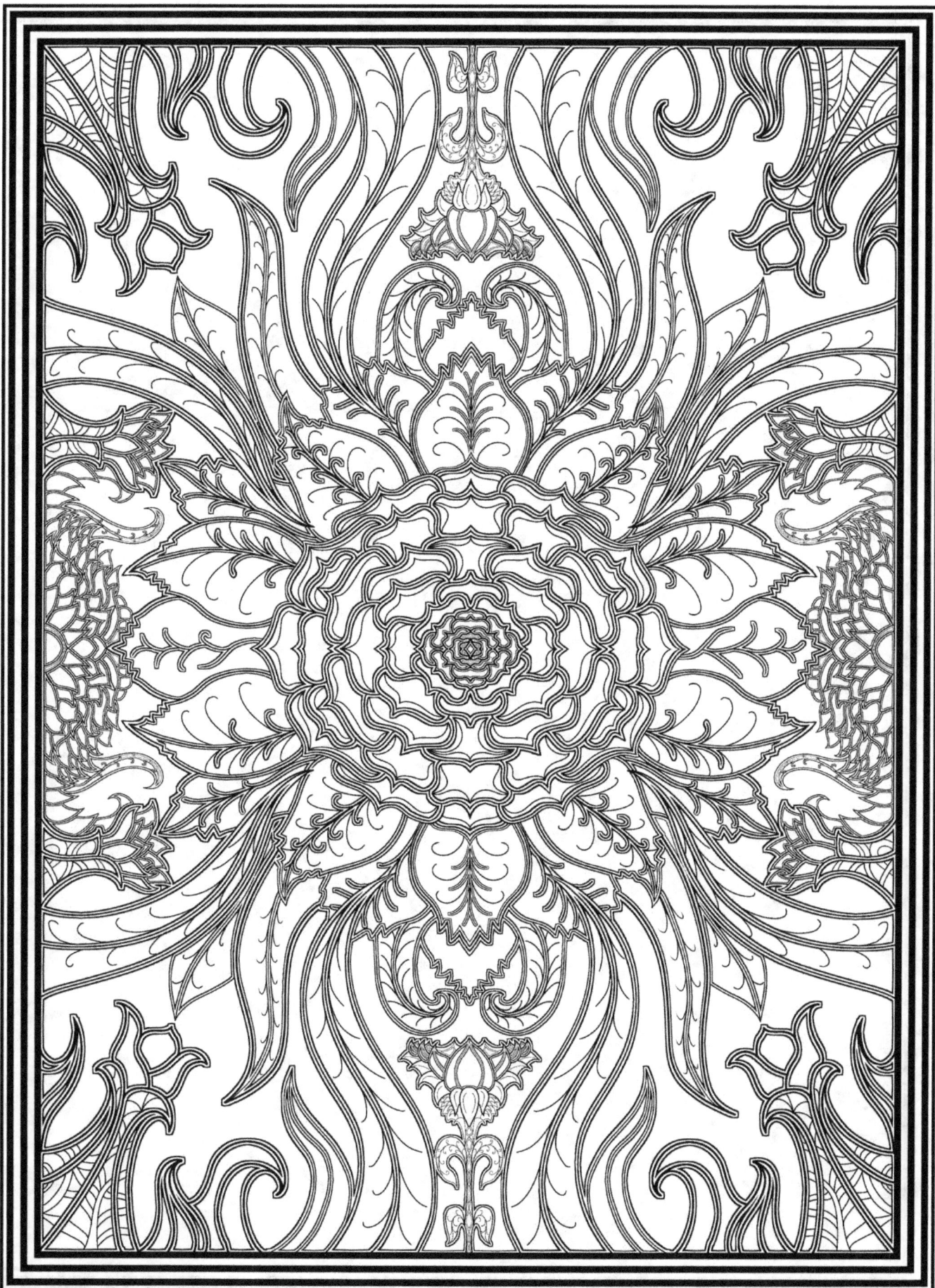

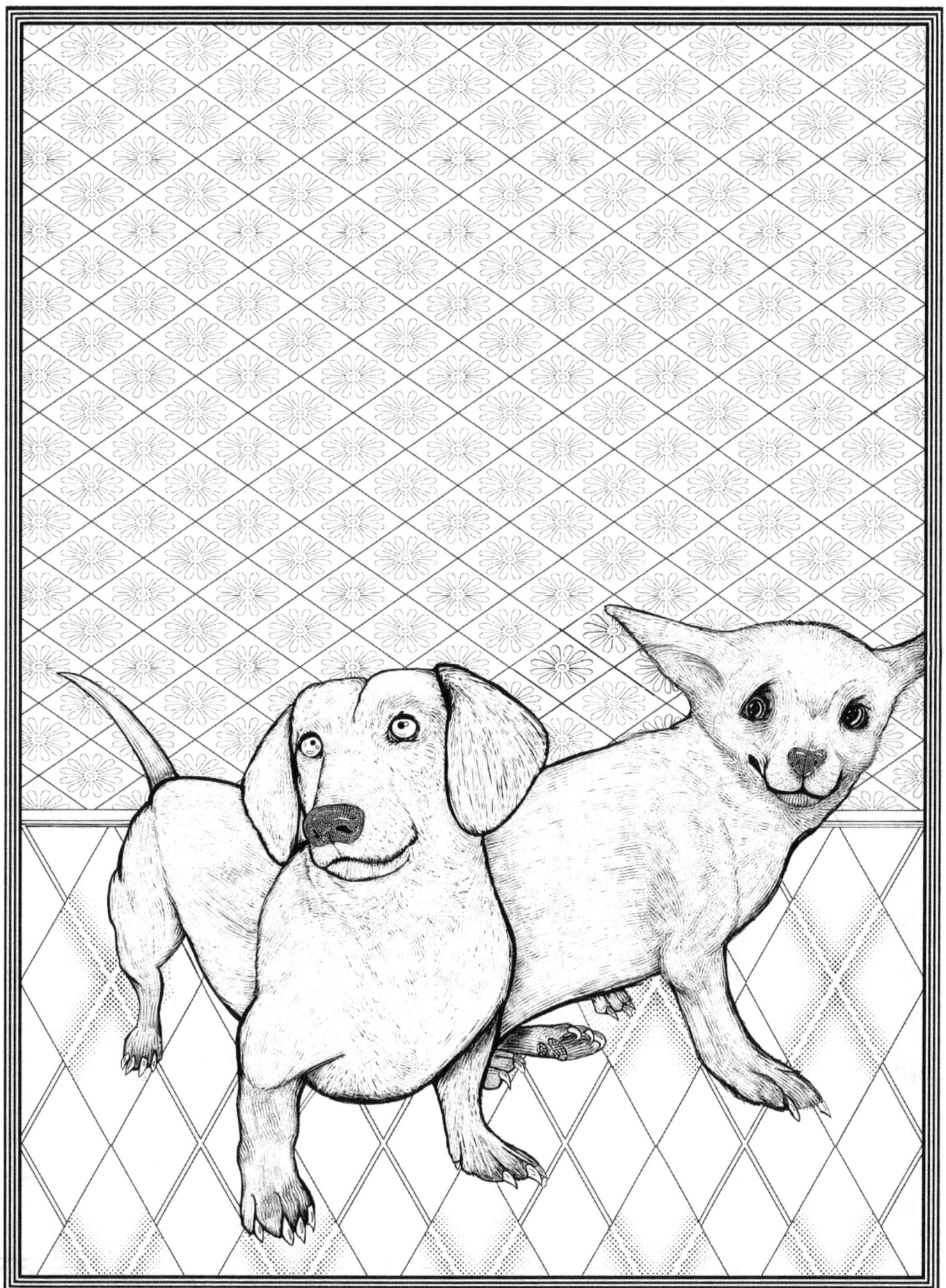

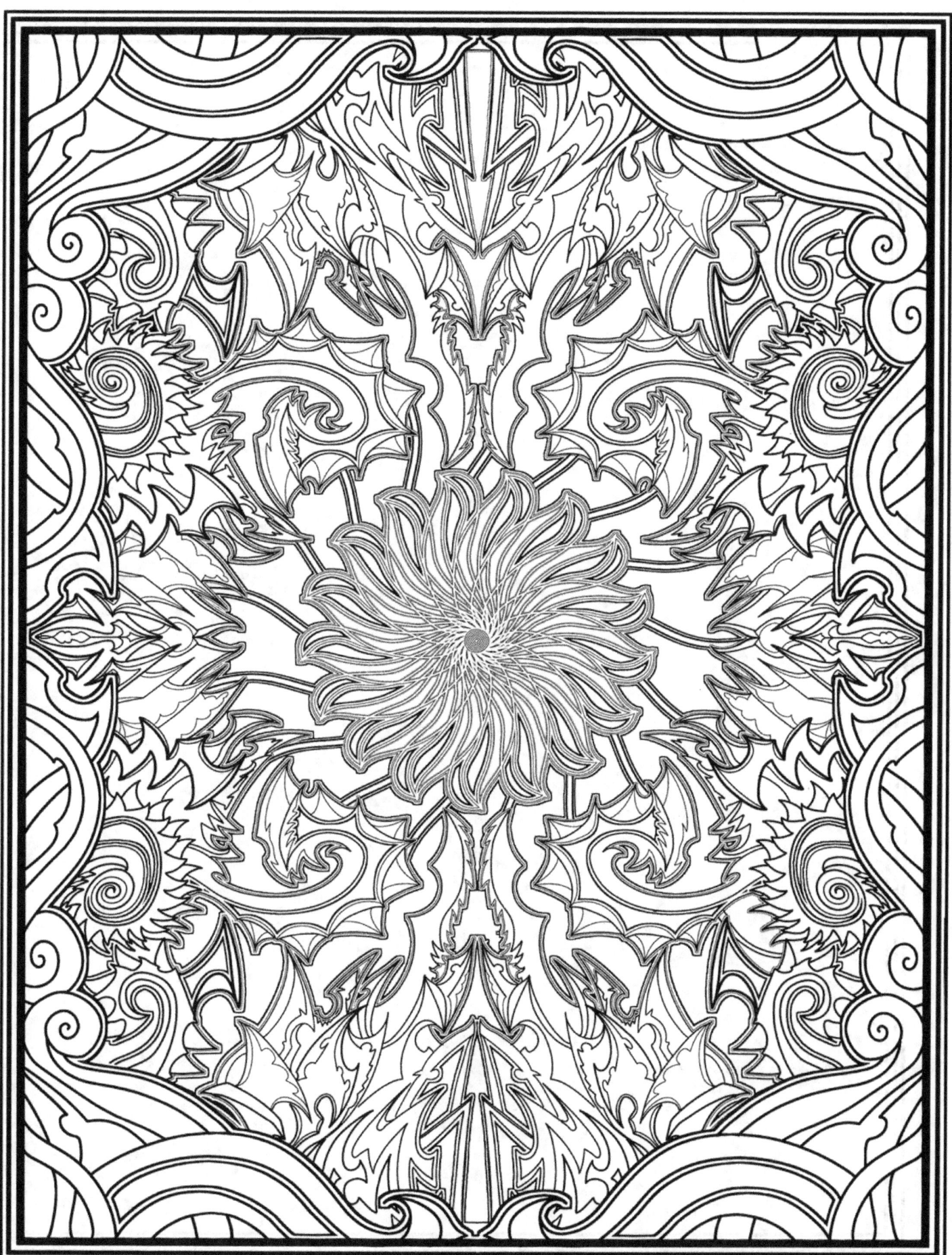

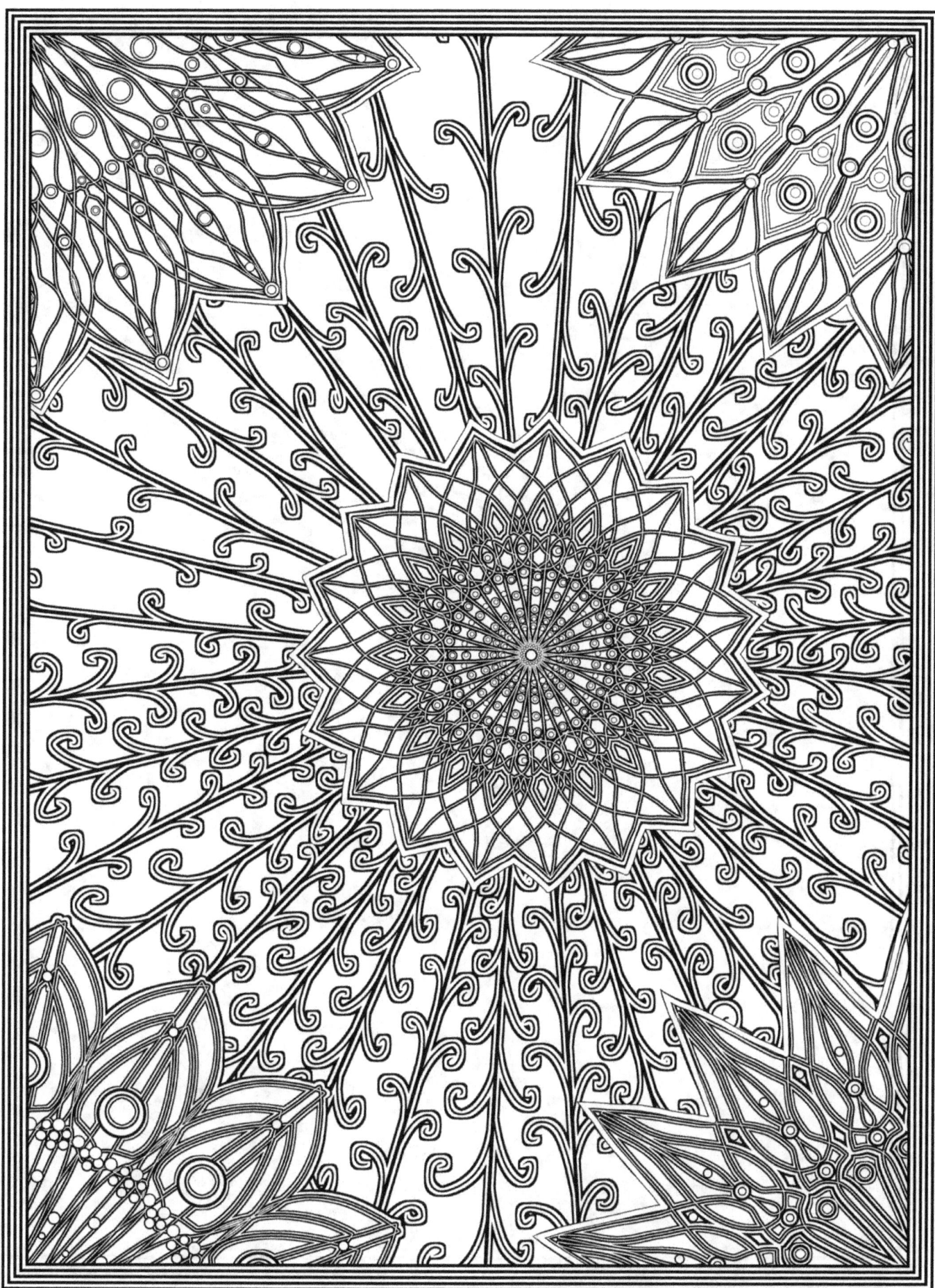

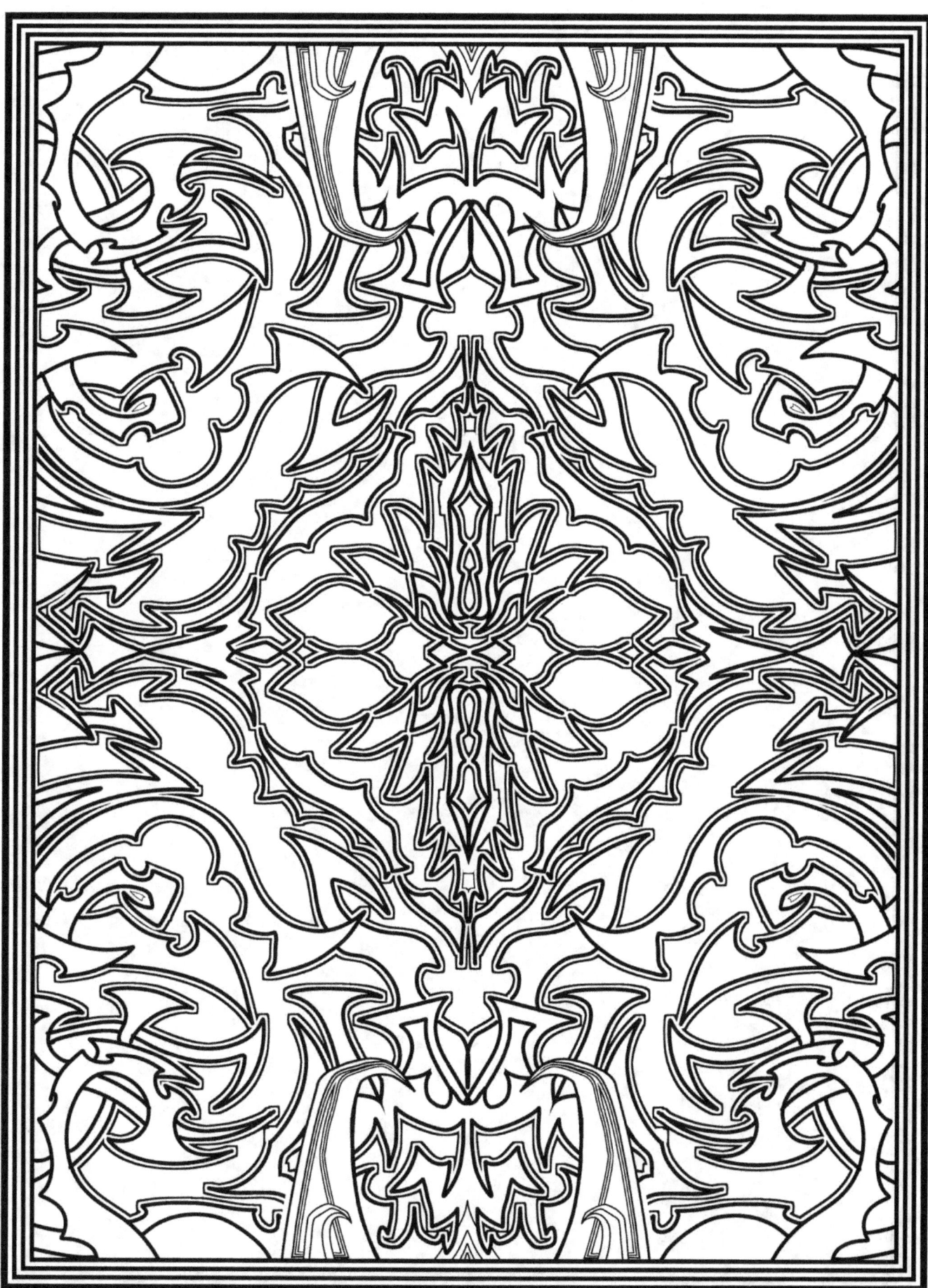

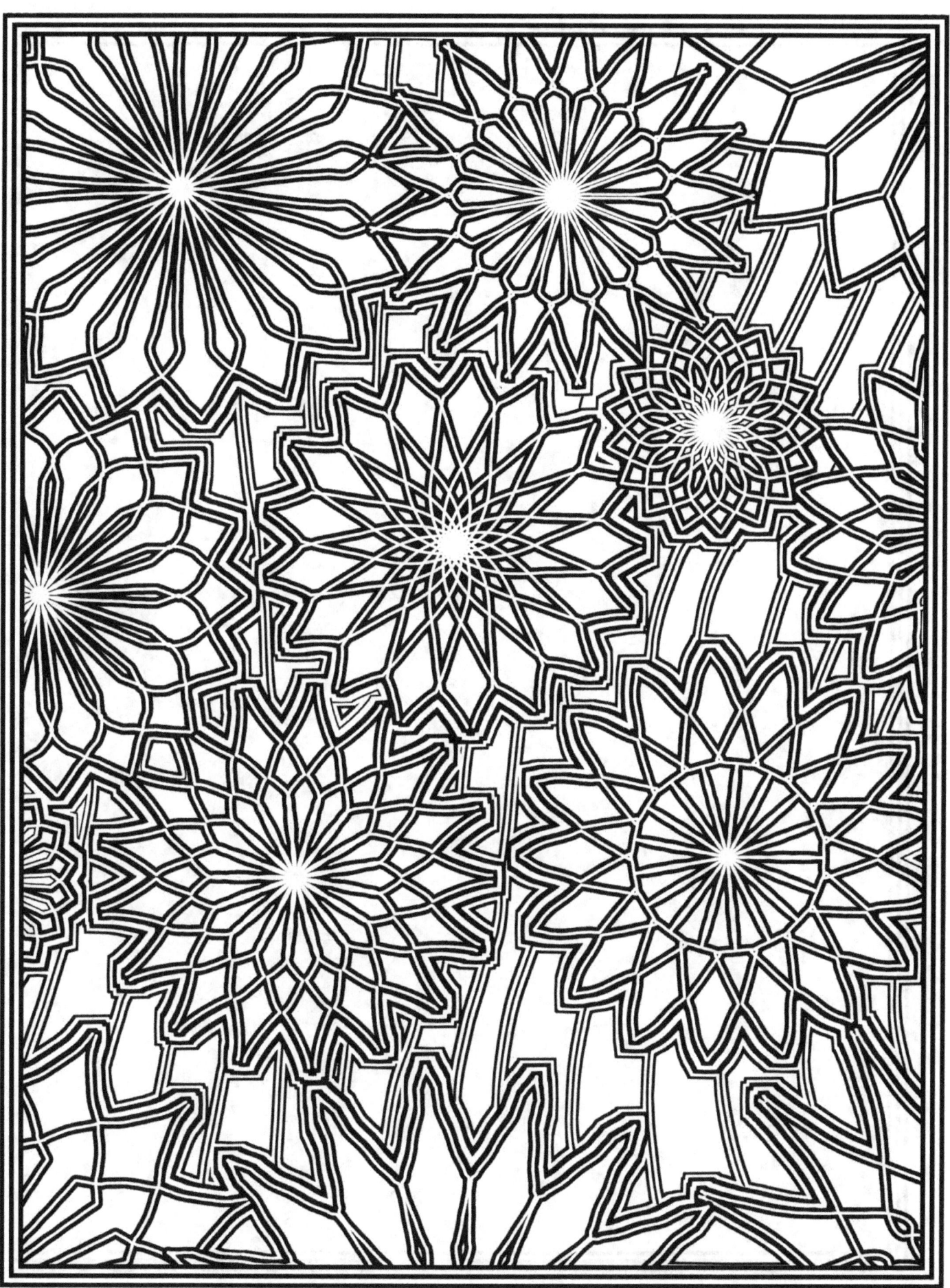

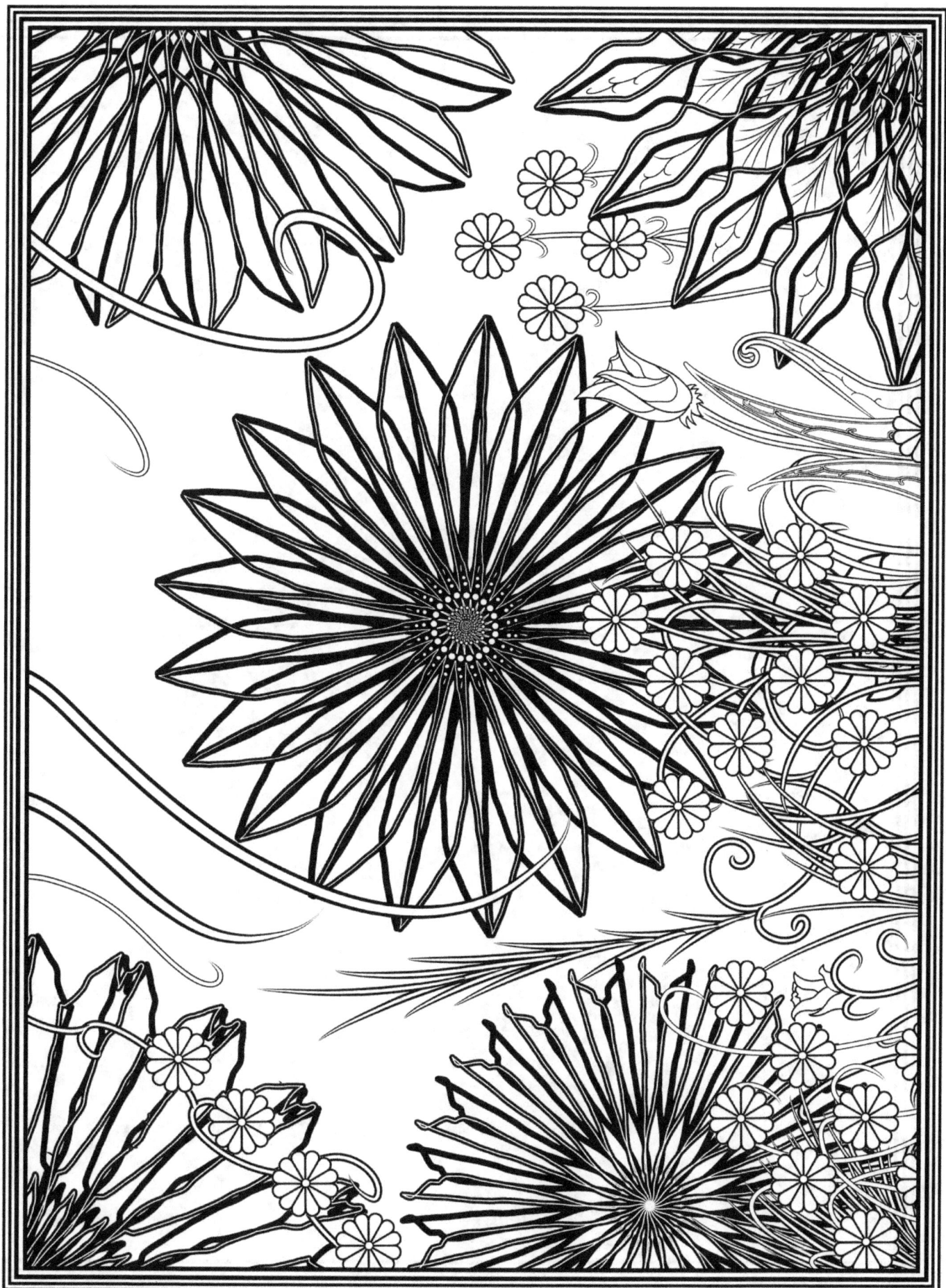

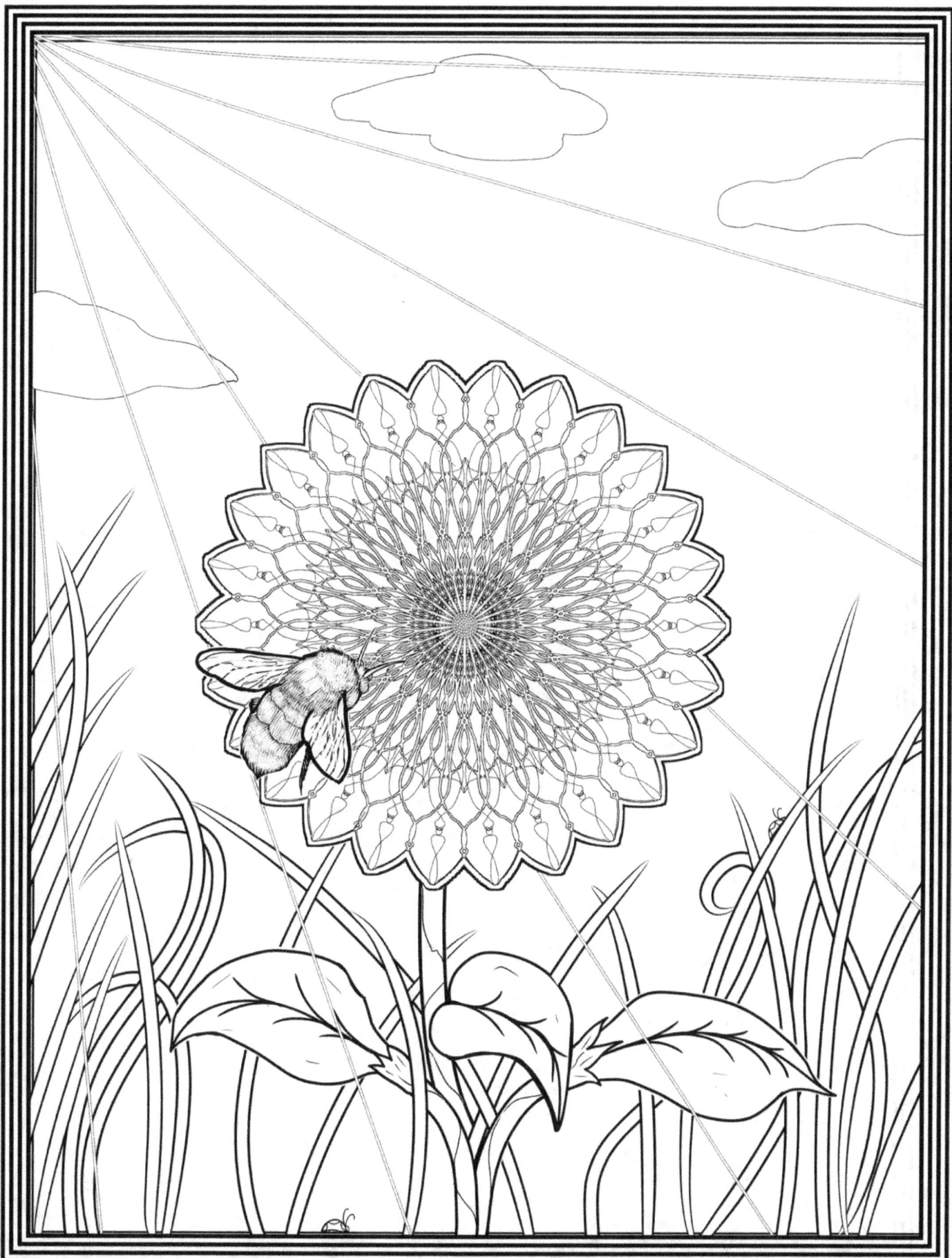

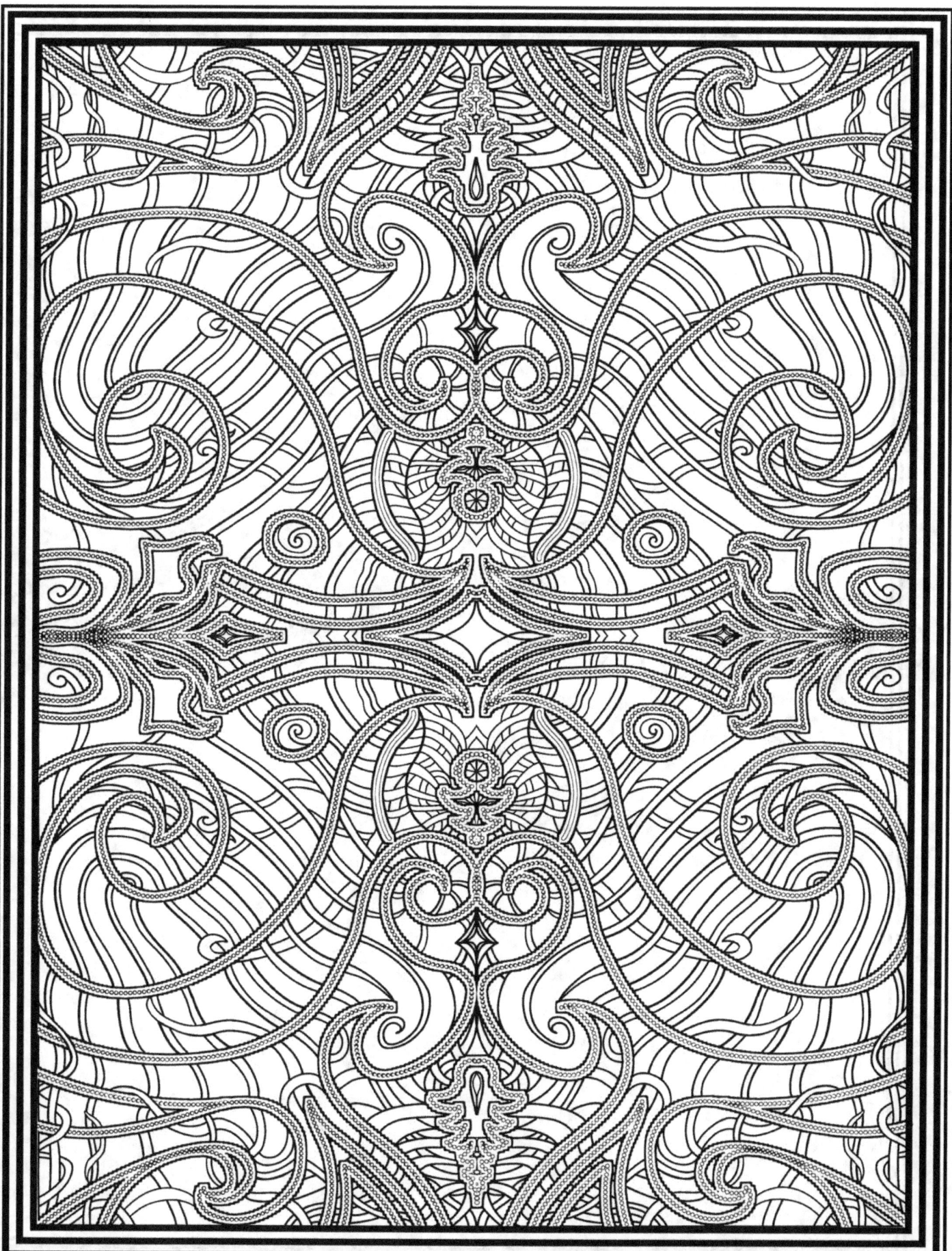

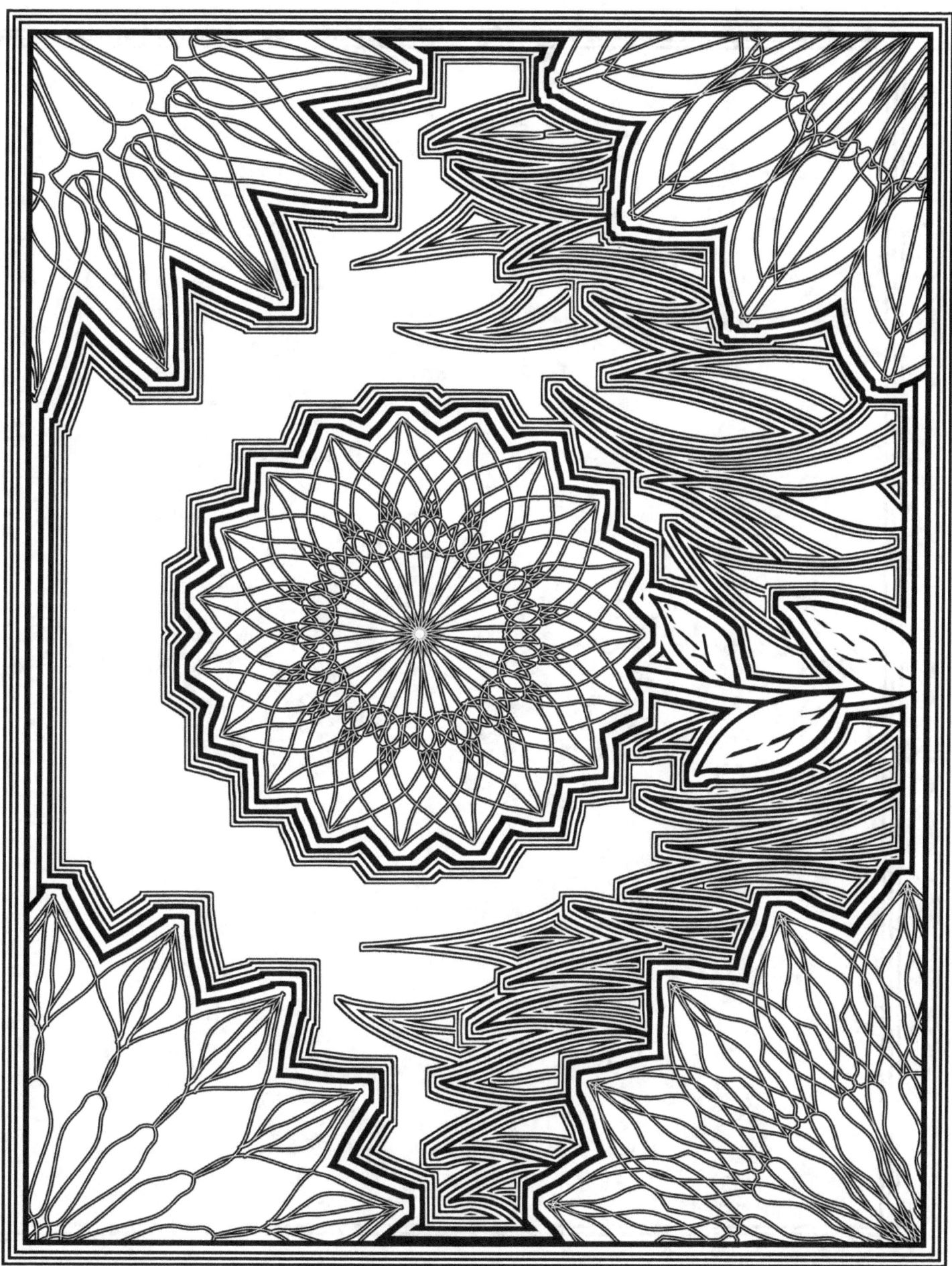

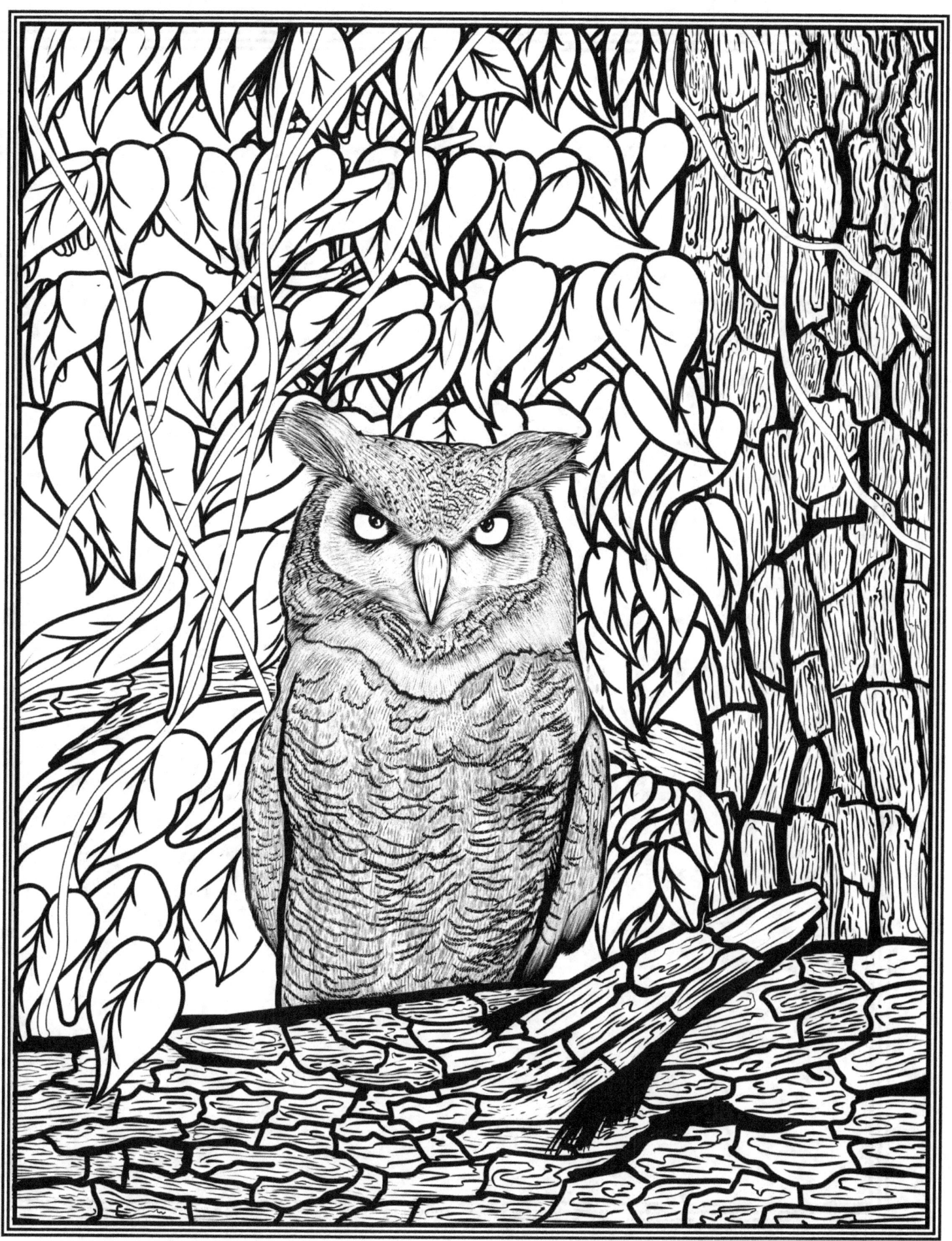

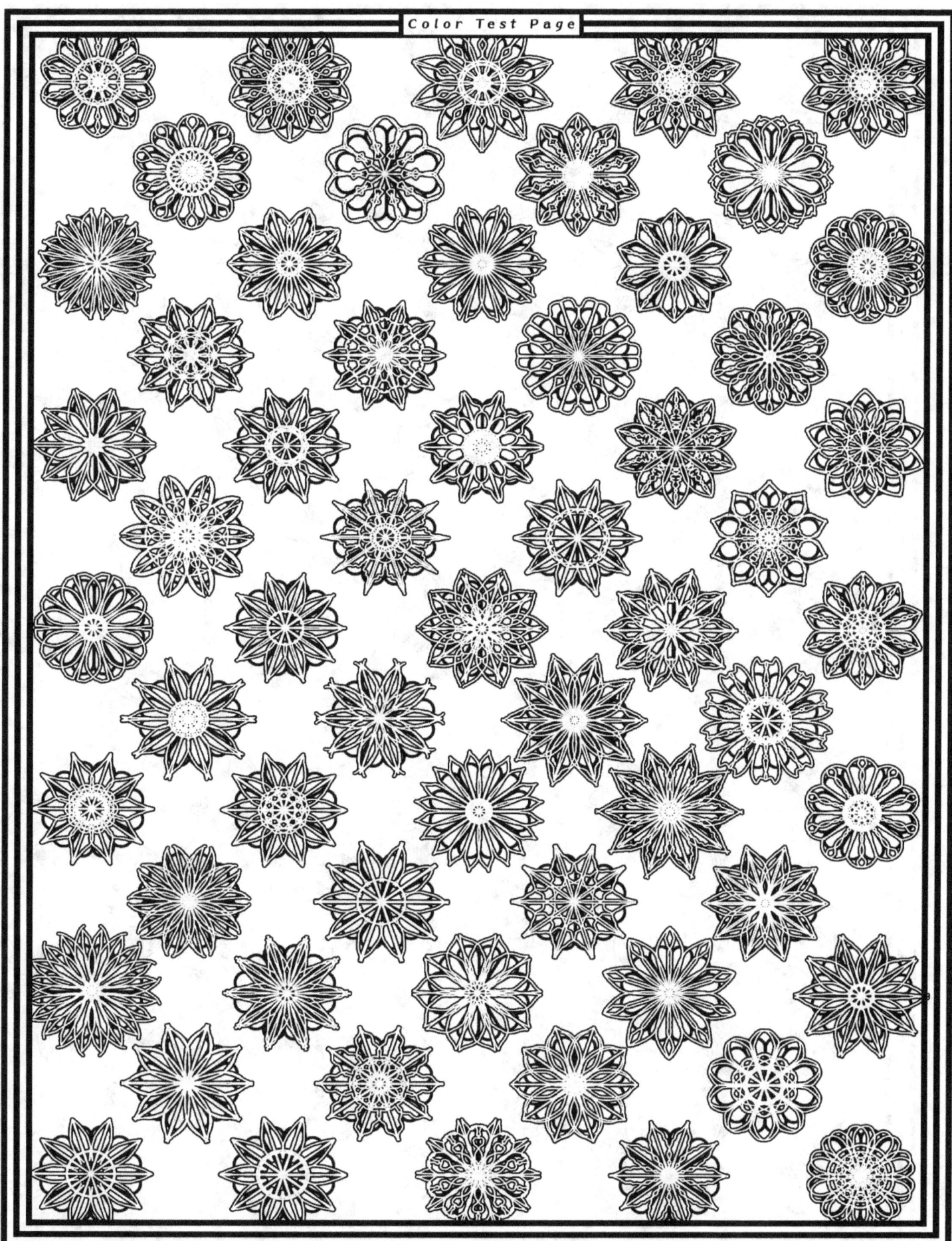

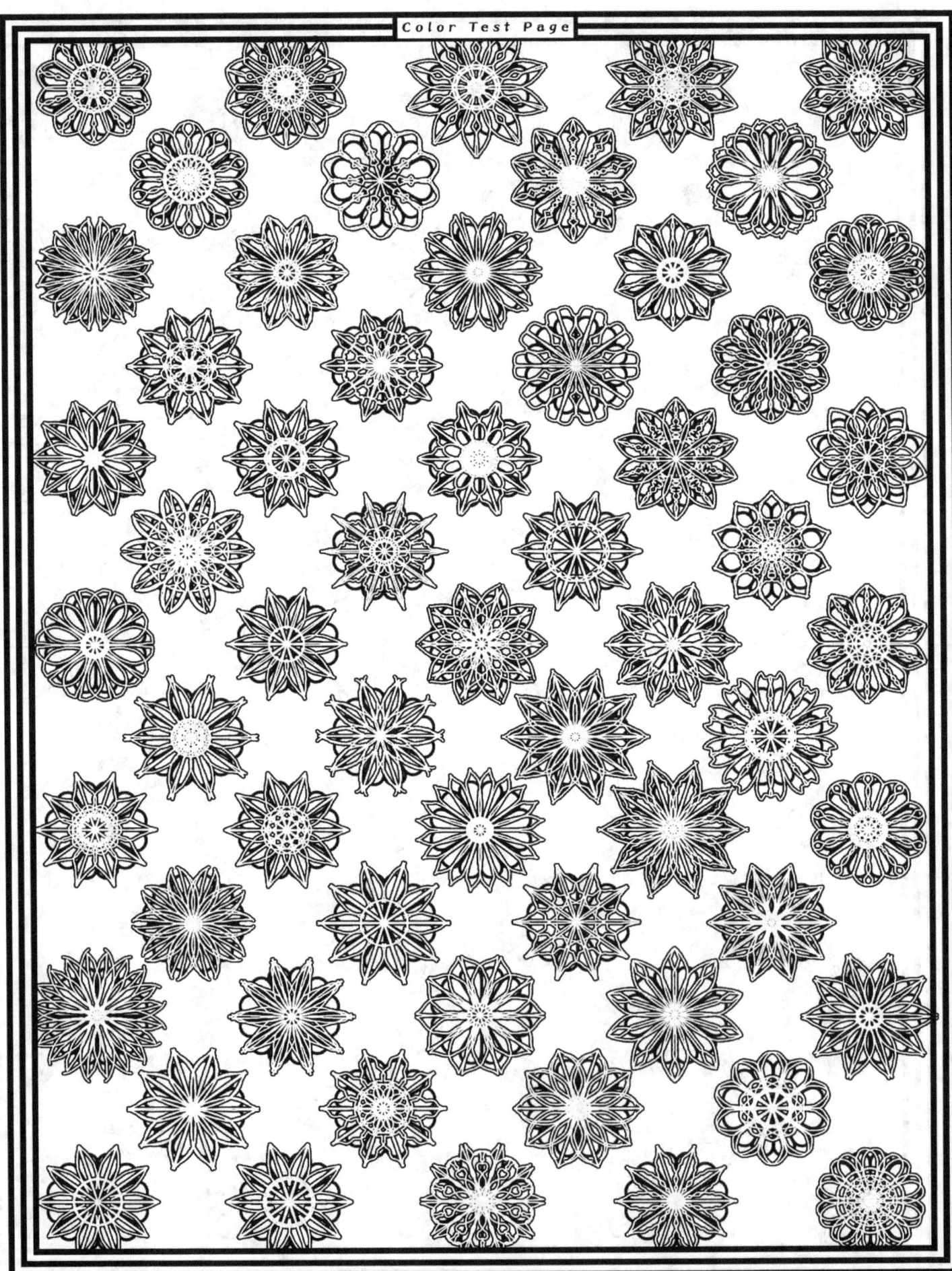

Color Test Page

Color Test Page

Color Test Page

Color Test Page

Color Test Page.

Color Test Page.

www.ingramcontent.com/pod-product-compliance
Lightning Source LLC
Chambersburg PA
CBHW081748220526
45468CB00008B/2292